Breastfeeding ... naturally

The Australian Breastfeeding Association's guide to breastfeeding — from birth to weaning

third edition • edited by Jill Day

Australian Breastfeeding Association

National Library of Australia
Cataloguing-in-Publication data:
Breastfeeding ... naturally
3rd edition
Includes index
ISBN 978-1-921001-57-4

1. Breastfeeding. 2. Motherhood. I. Day, Jill.
II. Australian Breastfeeding Association. III. Title.
649.33
Edited by Jill Day
for the Australian Breastfeeding Association

First published 1996 (edited by Jane Cafarella)
Second edition 2004, Minor revision 2006, 2008, 2009
Third edition 2011, Minor revision 2012, 2014, 2015

Published and distributed by
Australian Breastfeeding Association
(formerly Nursing Mothers' Association of Australia)
1818–1822 Malvern Road, East Malvern VIC 3145

Printed in Australia by Finsbury Green *finsburygreen.com.au*
This publication has been printed by an ISO 14001 environmental management system (EMS) and ISO 9001 quality management system (QMS) certified printer using vegetable based inks and a 100% alcohol free printing process. It is manufactured using an independently audited carbon neutral process.

Cover design and book layout by Artemiss Keyhani

> *The baby is referred to as he/him and she/her in alternate chapters in this book.*

Breastfeeding
... naturally

Australian Breastfeeding Association

TELEPHONE: (03) 9885 0855
(outside Australia +61 3 98850855)

FACSIMILE: (03) 9885 0866
(outside Australia +61 3 98850866)

EMAIL: *info@breastfeeding.asn.au*

WEBSITE: *breastfeeding.asn.au*

AUSTRALIAN BREASTFEEDING ASSOCIATION

Vision   Breastfeeding is recognised as important by all Australians and is culturally normal.

Mission   As Australia's leading authority on breastfeeding, we support, educate and advocate for a breastfeeding inclusive society.

Breastfeeding Helpline

24-hours a day. 7-days a week. Australia-wide.

For assistance outside of Australia, please visit: *breastfeeding.asn.au*

Breastfeeding Helpline

1800 mum 2 mum

1800 686 268

The Breastfeeding Helpline is supported by funding from the Australian Government.

Contents

Contents

Contents

INTRODUCTION

We know that breastfeeding is important for babies, mothers and families. Breastmilk provides a unique blend of ingredients that only the human body can produce, in the combination and quantity that your growing baby needs. The more we find out about breastmilk, the more we know that it is important to help every mother to breastfeed her baby, and for our society to encourage the use of human milk banks for babies and mothers who need extra support.

Breastfeeding ... naturally was first published in 1996 and this third edition continues the unique combination of up-to-date research, evidence-based information and current resources together with the wisdom, insights and experience of generations of parents.

In these pages you will find the information you need and suggestions that will help: preparation while you are pregnant; baby's first moments at the breast; establishing breastfeeding; problem solving; learning about family foods; sleep; weaning and much more. *Breastfeeding ... naturally* is Australia's most popular book on breastfeeding. The Australian Breastfeeding Association (ABA) has almost 50 years of experience providing breastfeeding support and information for mothers and families. Having this book by your side is like having a trusted friend to help you.

We also know that not all of your questions will have simple answers. Breastfeeding, just like anything else that you and your baby learn, can have its challenges. Sometimes you also need hugs, reassurance and the knowledge that loving support, persistence and taking things a day at a time will get you through.

Your baby will have love, breastfeeding, nurturing. This book adds some more of what you need — information, resources, experience and support for your choices. Only you are able to make the decisions that work for you and your baby.

Sometimes, you will need more than the information in this book. If you need medical support, we encourage you to visit a health professional skilled in lactation who can assess both you and your baby. ABA provides extra information, resources and internet forums on our website. Our members' magazine, *Essence,* has regular parenting and breastfeeding articles. Counselling is available through the national Breastfeeding Helpline 1800 686 268 (1800 mum 2 mum) and for members by email. At local groups around Australia you can find answers to the next questions you have and friendships that will enrich your life as a parent. By becoming a member of ABA you not only gain the benefits of membership but also have opportunities to share your own experiences of breastfeeding with other mothers.

I hope you enjoy breastfeeding, a relationship that is close to your heart in so many ways. As you welcome your baby into your arms and your family, I hope that this book will become a companion on your breastfeeding journey.

Warmly
Querida David
ABA President 2008–2011

CHAPTER 1

A commitment to breastfeeding

What does 'breast is best' actually mean?

What the World Health Organization (WHO) says about breastfeeding:

Over the past decades, evidence for the importance of breastfeeding and recommendations for practice have continued to increase. WHO can say with full confidence that breastfeeding reduces child mortality and has health benefits that extend into adulthood. Exclusive breastfeeding for the first 6 months of life is the recommended way of feeding infants, followed by continued breastfeeding with appropriate complementary foods for up to 2 years and beyond.

Breastmilk is the natural first food for babies. It provides all the energy and nutrients that the infant needs for the first 6 months of life. It continues to provide at least half or more of a child's nutritional needs during the second half of the first year and up to one-third during the second year of life.

Your interest in breastfeeding may have come from watching and listening to family and other breastfeeding mothers, or from what you have picked up in books or in the media. Perhaps it simply feels right for you and your baby. Whatever your reasons for deciding to breastfeed, you can be confident that your instincts are right. Breastmilk is the ideal food for your baby and a convenient and pleasurable choice for you.

Perhaps the best answer if someone asks if you intend to breastfeed is: *'Naturally!'*

What does 'breast is best' actually mean?

Almost everyone has heard the term 'breast is best'. Most of us know that breastfeeding protects a baby's immune system, but we don't always know the other reasons why it is 'best'. Actually breast isn't best. That suggests that there is something almost as good to compare it with. This is not the case. Breastfeeding is simply normal. It's the way nature intended us to feed our babies.

We now have an avalanche of research on the value of breastfeeding — far too much to go into detail in this chapter, but here's a start.

The more you know about how important breastfeeding is and why it makes a difference to your baby and to you, the more likely you are to make truly informed decisions. This is very important if you're having a few problems and are wondering if it's worth the effort.

Breastfeeding creates an irreplaceable bond between mother and baby
Breastfeeding is not just a feeding method; it's a nurturing relationship between you and your baby which is intensely fulfilling emotionally.
- Touch is a basic human need. Skin-to-skin contact during breastfeeding gives your baby a sense of security and wellbeing. He can feel the warmth and softness of your skin and hear your heartbeat.
- As you breastfeed, the release of relaxing hormones (prolactin — the 'mothering' hormone, and oxytocin — the 'love' hormone) helps you to bond with your child and feel good.
- As your baby grows, he will use breastfeeding as a time to get to know you — gazing into your eyes, stroking your breast, maybe playing with your hair and clothing. These moments of joy make the hard work of mothering worthwhile.

Knowing that my baby was growing and healthy, and we had achieved that together — with my breastmilk alone, was the most amazing feeling.

Your breastmilk is the perfect match for your baby
Each mother's milk is unique.
- Your breastmilk is a living fluid, constantly changing to meet your baby's needs as he grows. It is a unique match with your baby for as long as you breastfeed.
- Your breastmilk contains anti-infective factors that help protect your baby from any illnesses/germs you are both exposed to. The mix of anti-infective properties and nutrients changes from feed to feed.

Breastmilk is important for the normal development of your baby's immune system
The immunological properties of breastmilk protect your baby for as long as breastfeeding continues, whether this is weeks, months or years.
- When your baby is born, his immune system is not mature. It develops over the first 9–12 months. Breastfeeding protects your baby during this time. Without it, he is more likely to get sick.
- The colostrum your new baby receives in the first few days provides special protection as he makes the change from the safety of the womb to his new world.
- The longer your baby continues to breastfeed, the more protection it offers him. This protection continues as long as you continue to breastfeed.

Breastmilk protects your baby against illness — now and later
Breastmilk is essentially a preventative medicine as well as a source of nutrition.
- Breastfeeding provides protection against digestive and respiratory illnesses. It can also protect against urinary tract infections well after weaning.
- Babies who are formula-fed have a significantly greater risk of contracting gastroenteritis and, conversely, are more likely to become constipated.
- Premature babies who are formula-fed are at significantly higher risk of necrotising enterocolitis and sepsis.
- Illnesses such as middle ear infections and eczema, that have come to be regarded as part of the normal trials of childhood, are much more common in babies who are formula-fed.
- Children who have been formula-fed have a higher incidence of overweight and obesity in childhood and adulthood.
- Breastfed babies have a lower risk of sudden infant death syndrome (SIDS).

No-one is saying that breastfed babies never get sick. However, even in affluent countries like Australia, formula-fed babies are many times more likely to become ill. If breastfed babies do become ill, it is often milder and they usually recover quicker.

Breastmilk has all the ingredients needed for your baby to grow

Human milk has a complex mix of ingredients that not only nourish and protect your baby but also help to regulate his growth and his metabolism in many subtle ways.

- Breastmilk alone provides a complete, balanced diet for your baby for his first 6 months. It satisfies both his hunger and his thirst. It continues to be the most important part of his diet throughout his first year.
- Breastmilk has just the right amount of protein, fats, salts, sugars and other nutrients.
- Your baby easily absorbs the calcium in breastmilk.
- The iron absorbed through breastmilk is enough to maintain normal reserves for at least 6 months.

- The small, soft curds of breastmilk are easily processed by your baby's sensitive digestive system.
- The action of breastfeeding supports the normal process of eyesight, speech and jaw development.

Breastfeeding gives me a sense of fulfilment beyond compare. It is something only I can do for my baby. I stroke her hair and pat her softly and talk to her as she nestles her face against my breast.

Breastfeeding gives your baby a head start
Breastfeeding enhances babies' intelligence and emotional wellbeing.
- Breastfed babies have the best chance of reaching their full IQ potential.
- The act of breastfeeding itself as well as the fatty acids in breastmilk and the way they combine with other components are important for brain development. This combination can't be copied. Simply adding some of them to formula doesn't mean they will act in the same way as they do in breastmilk.

Breastmilk is clean, safe and always on tap
Breastmilk is delivered straight from breast to baby.
- It's always there when you need it, it never runs out and it's always at just the right temperature.
- There is no risk of contamination and no storage problems. If you're bottle-feeding, there's always the worry that you'll either run out of formula or that it will go off in the heat.
- Your breastfed baby's wellbeing will not be threatened by power failures, natural disasters or emergencies.
- It makes life so much easier if you can go out with your baby without having to worry about where his next feed is coming from. You can stay out as long as you like. You don't have to stress about getting home to make up the next bottle. You can breastfeed your baby anywhere, any time.

Breastfeeding saves money
Every dollar counts once a new baby comes into the house.
- Breastfeeding costs nothing apart from what you might spend on a little extra food for yourself. Breastfeeding mothers usually feel a bit hungrier than before.
- Bottle-feeding isn't cheap. There's the cost of the infant formula, plus the bottles, teats and all the equipment needed to make it safe. Of course, parents put their baby's needs ahead of their own when it comes to spending, but many families

struggle to find enough money to buy formula and the necessary equipment.

- Another expense rarely taken into account is the medical bills when a baby becomes ill. It's been estimated that hospitalisation rates for children in their first year could be halved if all babies were fully breastfed for at least 4 months.

'I'm still nursing, and I think it gives you superhuman powers.'
(Singer Gwen Stefani, talking about breastfeeding her 6-month-old son.)

Breastfeeding is good for mothers too
Just as breastfeeding is important for babies, so it is important for mothers.

- Women who don't breastfeed have an increased risk of ovarian and breast cancer.
- Breastfeeding helps get you back in shape. It's nature's way of helping your uterus to return to its pre-pregnant state.
- A formula-feeding mother will usually take longer to return to her pre-pregnancy figure. Breastfeeding can help you lose some of that pregnancy weight.
- Your periods usually don't return for many months if you breastfeed your baby exclusively. Breastfeeding can act as a contraceptive during this time. See Chapter 11 for more information.
- Middle of the night feeds are much easier when your baby doesn't have to wait for you to heat up a bottle. You'll both be asleep again much faster and the rest of the family's sleep is less likely to be disturbed.
- With nappies taking up more of your day than you ever thought possible, you'll be pleased to know that a breastfed baby's poo definitely smells better than that of a formula-fed baby.
- Knowing that you alone are able to provide all the nutrition that your baby needs for the first 6 months of life is incredibly satisfying.
- Breastfeeding can be very liberating and make you feel confident and powerful as a woman.

Breastfeeding has a global impact
Breastmilk is possibly the 'greenest' food your child will ever have.

- Breastmilk is produced at little cost to the physical environment. Infant-formula-feeding uses energy and resources. Breastfeeding can save our country millions of dollars in imports.
- Breastfeeding also saves our country millions of dollars in health costs. Based on Australian research, the annual cost of the hospitalisation of prematurely weaned babies alone is many millions of dollars.

- Despite the World Health Organization International Code of Marketing of Breast-milk Substitutes (known as the WHO Code), the promotion and marketing of formula is still causing the death of babies in both the developed and developing world. Your decision to breastfeed your own child shows solidarity with all mothers who are striving to do so, sometimes against great odds. By breastfeeding, you are supporting other breastfeeding women around the world.

Why do I breastfeed? I breastfeed because it is how human females were designed to nurture their young. I breastfeed because it allows me precious close time with my daughter. I breastfeed because it ensures my daughter is getting optimum nutrition and antibodies and will have a smaller chance of contracting major diseases. I breastfeed because it is convenient, portable and easy and because she can have access to it anytime she wants. If I wanted to go out without her I could express enough milk for her to drink. I breastfeed because it eases her discomforts. It nurtures her soul as well as her body. It offers a warm, safe and peaceful place to be when she is sad or hurts herself.

CHAPTER 2

Truths about breastfeeding

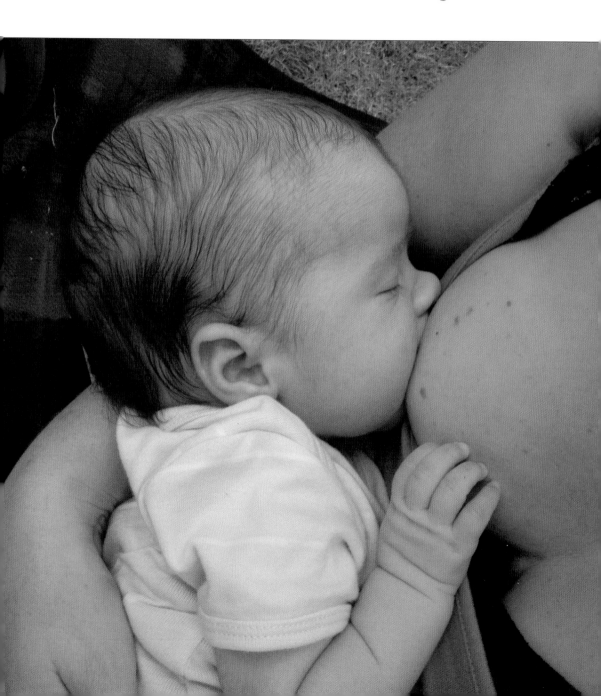

There is a common misconception, even today, that the only difference between bottle-feeding and breastfeeding is the container.

The value of breastfeeding to the health and wellbeing of the Australian community is widely accepted. The visions of the Australian National Breastfeeding Strategy are:

- Australia is a nation in which breastfeeding is protected, promoted, supported and valued by the whole of society.
- Breastfeeding is viewed as the biological norm for infant and young child feeding.
- Mothers, families, health professionals and other caregivers are fully informed about the value of breastfeeding.

There are many common myths and misconceptions about breastfeeding. Sorting fact from fiction will give you the confidence to ignore wrong advice and continue to breastfeed successfully.

Truth #1 'Breastfeeding and bottle-feeding are not equal choices'

Breastfeeding is a vital part of the reproductive process — the final stage of the conception-pregnancy-birth cycle. Nature programs our bodies to produce breastmilk for our new babies. Thinking about breastfeeding like this makes it a reproductive right rather than a consumer decision.

As long as infant feeding is seen purely as a 'choice' made by an individual woman from two equal options, we make her solely responsible for carrying through with that choice. If she wants to breastfeed, it's up to her to make it work. This frees the rest of society from providing the systems and support that would give all women a real chance of breastfeeding for as long as they wish. But if breastfeeding was seen as a 'right', then society would work harder to improve maternity services, train all health professionals in breastfeeding knowledge and provide workplace and childcare programs. Services like this would give many more women the support they need to work through breastfeeding challenges and continue to breastfeed their babies.

Truth #2 'There is a huge difference between breastmilk and modern infant formula'

Even today, many people mistakenly believe that the only difference between infant formula and breastfeeding is the container — breastmilk comes in a breast, formula in a bottle. Having the breast always there, whenever baby needs a feed, is very convenient. However, some people see the bottle as convenient too, because others can feed the baby. But babies are meant to be kept close to their mothers in the early weeks. The close body contact of breastfeeding helps regulate the baby's bodily functions. It enhances emotional development and family bonding.

> **Breastmilk is designed to meet the changing needs of each baby. It changes with her age, stage of development, frequency of feeds and the time of day. It creates antibodies against illnesses that the mother or baby may be exposed to. Formula does not adapt in this way and so can't protect and nourish your baby like your breastmilk does.**

Breastmilk also contains a unique mix of fatty acids which encourage optimal brain development and protect against illnesses. No formula has ever been able to copy these unique qualities of breastmilk.

The reality is that when you compare formula with breastmilk, they are not equal. Science may have made some improvements to formulas, and modern hygiene (in developed countries) makes their use less risky. However, there is no formula that comes close to the life-giving and life-saving properties of breastmilk, a fact that the infant formula companies cannot dispute. Breastmilk and formula are not equal.

Truth #3 'Promoting breastfeeding supports all mothers'

Women are bombarded with health messages about what we should eat, how much we should exercise or how we should manage our own and our children's health. Most of the time, we don't resent someone telling us what's important to our health.

Yet many women passionately resent being told that breastfeeding makes a difference to their health and that of their baby. Somehow the breastfeeding message, rather than being pro-mother and pro-baby, can be seen as anti-mother and anti-choice.

Breastfeeding advocates want to make it possible for all mothers and babies to experience all that breastfeeding has to offer, but they do not want to make bottle-feeding mothers feel guilty. Breastfeeding is a basic human right and that right is worth fighting for. All mothers deserve good technical advice and support to breastfeed.

The vast majority of Australian mothers start off breastfeeding. Those who choose formula-feeding right from the start have, we hope, made an informed decision and are comfortable with that decision. However, for too many women, choosing to feed their babies infant formula is not a choice, but the result of conflicting and incorrect advice and a lack of support.

Organisations like the Australian Breastfeeding Association (ABA) aren't there to make bottle-feeding mothers feel bad. They're there to offer you as much help as you need to make breastfeeding work for you. They can offer you non-judgemental support if things don't go as planned.

Truth #4 'Breastfeeding gives you freedom'

Our society places a strong focus on the rights and needs of the individual. It's hardly surprising that the thought of having someone totally dependent on us can seem scary.

Parenting, particularly mothering where much more physical intimacy is involved, is extremely hard work. Babies are human beings with very real and very immediate needs — none of which they are capable of meeting without your help.

In the early weeks, whether you breastfeed or bottle-feed, you'll spend a lot of your day with your baby in your arms. As time goes on, you'll have more time for yourself. In the meantime, you and your partner will probably be sharing the physical load. If you're lucky, you'll be able to call on both your families so that you can have some 'time-out' together.

As a breastfeeding mother, you will spend a lot of time literally attached to your baby. You might be surprised to find it's mostly a joy to cuddle and care for her. Breastfeeding allows you space to put aside less important things while you and your baby enjoy each other. It also gives you a chance to sit and rest.

Truth #5 'Partners have an important role when their baby is breastfed'

Sometimes, partners have mixed feelings about breastfeeding because they fear that they may miss out on bonding with their baby. Some are envious of the physical and emotional closeness between mother and child.

Parenting is not a competition for your baby's affection. Reassure your partner that while breastfeeding is vital for your baby's survival, holding, playing and loving are important too. Your partner can bond with your baby and enjoy skin-to-skin contact through cuddling, carrying, bathing and baby massage.

Talk about why you want to breastfeed and share your feelings with each other. Encourage your partner to read this book and to talk to other people whose partners have breastfed. Studies have shown that women are much more successful at breastfeeding when they have the backing of their partners. Assure your partner that the most helpful thing for you is support for your commitment to breastfeed. Partners may be surprised at the rewards they receive too. They often say that seeing their baby breastfeeding is an intensely emotional and proud experience.

Truth #6 'Breastfeeding is usually a pleasant and natural experience'

Embarrassment or negative feelings about our body's natural functions sometimes make us feel unsure about breastfeeding. Some people see breastmilk as waste matter that is eliminated from the body. Breastmilk is not related to waste products such as urine or sweat but is 'a living fluid', more like blood. Just as blood contains living cells which make our body work properly, so breastmilk carries nutrients and protective substances from mother to baby.

If it is not the milk, but the idea of somebody feeding from your breasts that disturbs you, then it can help to talk to other women about what breastfeeding actually feels like, particularly those who may have felt uncomfortable about it at first.

Some women who find the idea of breastfeeding off-putting, but try it anyway, are surprised to find it's not at all unpleasant. In fact, most women enjoy breastfeeding. Nature has designed it to be that way.

Truth #7 'Breastfeeding does not ruin your figure'

Comments like, 'You'll have boobs down to your waist!' are annoyingly common when you're breastfeeding, especially if you continue to feed your baby past early infancy. The idea that breastfeeding will ruin a woman's figure is not correct. Age, heredity, pregnancy and weight gain or loss all affect the way breasts change over time.

During pregnancy, your breasts prepare for breastfeeding by becoming larger. Your nipples and areola usually get darker and may become slightly larger as well. In the days after birth, your breasts become fuller and heavier as your milk 'comes in'. Over the next few weeks or so, they return to about the size they were during pregnancy and stay that way until you wean your baby. Then they are likely to return to their pre-pregnant size. Whether or not you breastfeed, they probably won't be quite as 'perky' as they were before you were pregnant. Pregnancy has changed them.

A wonderful thing about breastfeeding is that whatever your pre-pregnancy figure or breast size, your breasts will adapt to meet the needs of your baby.

Truth #8 'Breastfeeding does not hurt'

If a baby is attached properly and sucking well, breastfeeding does not hurt. In fact, for most mothers it is a pleasurable experience. However, some nipple pain which ceases after the initial attachment is common is the early weeks as you adjust to breastfeeding. If the pain continues beyond the initial attachment or your nipples look creased after feeds or show any signs of damage, seek help. Any problems can usually be solved quickly and easily.

Breastfeeding does not mean that a mother has to suffer for the good of her child. If you are feeling pain, there is something wrong and it should be attended to immediately. It is not easy to breastfeed your baby if you are in pain. This is the time to speak to your midwife, lactation consultant or ring a breastfeeding counsellor on the national Breastfeeding Helpline on 1800 686 268 for information and support.

Truth #9 'You don't need a special diet when you're breastfeeding'

The belief that breastfeeding women need to have a special diet or take dietary supplements is driven by companies trying to sell their products. Talk to your medical adviser about iodine which is the only supplement recommended by health authorities. It is needed by all pregnant and breastfeeding women. Other than this, you don't have to eat or drink any special foods. All you need to do is to follow your normal diet. However, you may find you are thirstier and hungrier than usual. Keep a glass of water and a healthy snack close by when you are breastfeeding.

Breastfeeding is designed so that your baby gets top priority when the nutrients are handed out, no matter what you eat. However, you are obviously going to feel (and look) better if you have a basic healthy diet. Some babies become fussy if their mother eats a lot of a particular food. Eating a wide variety of foods in moderation usually avoids this type of reaction. If you are concerned that your baby may be reacting to something you have eaten, call the national Breastfeeding Helpline on 1800 686 268 or visit your health professional. They can help you decide if there is a problem and how to manage it from there.

Truth #10 'It's OK to breastfeed in public'

Breastfeeding your baby is a normal and natural part of life. Babies have a right to be breastfed and mothers have the right to breastfeed. Most mothers work out where and how they can feed their babies when they are out, so that they feel comfortable. Chapter 9 has some practical suggestions.

By breastfeeding in public, women provide a positive image of breastfeeding. This helps promote its importance in our society and also helps other mothers feel more comfortable breastfeeding in public.

In 2001, ABA did a study of women's experiences of breastfeeding. Mothers said that what they wanted most was a society in which the importance of breastfeeding was universally acknowledged. They wanted to see a wider community understanding of how breastfeeding really works. Today, there is still a great deal of ignorance about breastfeeding. Many people, including health professionals, accept — and sadly pass on — information that is incorrect, contradictory or inconsistent. It takes a long time to change community attitudes and practices, but each mother and baby who enjoy breastfeeding is one small step forward.

CHAPTER 3

Preparing for breastfeeding

Learning-to-breastfeed classes

Hospitals and the Baby Friendly
Health Initiative

A breastfeeding mentor

Health professionals involved
in care of new mothers

Your partner

Maternity bras

Breast pumps

From the day you find out you're pregnant, you give a lot of thought to the birth of your baby. While this is important, it is equally — if not more — important to prepare for breastfeeding. Labour may last anything from 1 hour to 24 hours or more, but a successful breastfeeding relationship can last for months, if not years.

So how can you prepare? One way is to read about breastfeeding and watch and talk to breastfeeding mothers. The more you learn about breastfeeding, the more confident you will be and the more likely breastfeeding will work for you.

The internet is now one of the first places we go to for information. A good place to start is ABA's website: *breastfeeding.asn.au.* All its information is based on solid research and the experience of thousands of women.

A reality check ...
While you try to do all that you can to get ready for childbirth and breastfeeding, no-one can be totally prepared. No amount of reading or classes can prepare you for every possibility. Books and classes talk about the 'average' birth experience or the 'average' breastfeeding experience. Your baby is unique, so your breastfeeding relationship will be unique. The trick is to be able to adapt when things don't go by the book, to have enough basic knowledge, and to know when it's time to ask for help.

Learning-to-breastfeed classes

Most maternity hospitals run classes to prepare you for the birth of your baby. All antenatal programs have a breastfeeding education component.

ABA offers Breastfeeding Education Classes in many localities across the country. The class, which usually runs over 3–4 hours, gives expectant and new parents a real insight into caring for a breastfed baby. Even if you've already had your baby, it might be worth going along for a refresher and a confidence boost.

The program includes:
- how breastfeeding works and how breastmilk is made
- breast and nipple care, including common concerns
- how to attach and breastfeed a new baby
- what to expect from a new baby
- adjusting to parenthood and the effect of a new baby on the parents' relationship
- the role of the partner in breastfeeding
- information about expressing and storing breastmilk
- information about working and breastfeeding
- information about ABA and the support it provides to parents.

You will usually be able to watch a mother breastfeeding. You'll also be able to talk with her (and perhaps with her partner as well) and ask questions. Included in the cost of the class is a 1-year membership to ABA and its magazine, *Essence*. If you are already a member, you will only need to pay the additional fee to attend the class. ABA classes are friendly and informal, and refreshments and handouts are provided at no extra cost. To find a Breastfeeding Education Class near you, click on the link on ABA's website: *breastfeeding.asn.au>services>classes*.

Hospitals and the Baby Friendly Health Initiative

Most Australian women give birth in hospital — even some of those who plan a home birth. Your hospital will play a part in the establishment of breastfeeding. You should make it clear to those overseeing your care that you intend to breastfeed and that you want them to help you get off to a good start.

Having a baby has become increasingly 'medicalised'. Today, all women are routinely scanned and monitored. In the past, this was only done when a mother was 35 or older. The change is partly because technology is now used more widely across all areas of health care. But it is also a response to concerns that doctors and hospitals have about medical indemnity.

Whatever the reason, the end result is that women have become less confident in their ability to deliver and nurture a healthy baby. After the birth, all the monitoring stops. They are left to follow their instincts when feeding and caring for their baby. Trusting their body in this way can be a big leap for many mothers and takes a lot of self-confidence.

To assist maternity services to provide the best possible care for breastfeeding mothers, the World Health Organization (WHO) and the United Nations Children's Fund (UNICEF) produced the *Ten Steps to Successful Breastfeeding*. These steps require a hospital to:
1. Have a written breastfeeding policy that is routinely communicated to all health care staff.
2. Train all health care staff in skills necessary to implement this policy.
3. Inform all pregnant women about the benefits and management of breastfeeding.
4. Place babies in skin-to-skin contact with their mothers immediately following birth and encourage mothers to recognise when their babies are ready to breastfeed, offering help if needed.
5. Show mothers how to breastfeed and how to maintain lactation even if they should be separated from their infants.

6. Give newborn infants no food or drink other than breastmilk, unless medically indicated.
7. Practise rooming-in — allow mothers and infants to remain together — 24 hours a day.
8. Encourage breastfeeding on demand.
9. Give no artificial teats or pacifiers (also called dummies or soothers) to breastfeeding infants.
10. Foster the establishment of breastfeeding support and refer mothers on discharge from the facility.

Hospitals can formally demonstrate their commitment to breastfeeding by becoming accredited by the Baby Friendly Health Initiative. In Australia, accreditation is administered by the Australian College of Midwives.

In 2011, there were 77 Baby Friendly hospitals in Australia and others are working towards this status. Of all maternity hospitals, 23% are accredited, with one third of Australian babies born in a Baby Friendly hospital.

The policy in Baby Friendly hospitals is that a mother should decide how she will feed her baby, but her decision should be an informed one. Infant formula is not banned, but it is not supplied. Mothers who wish to use infant formula usually have to purchase and prepare their own. This includes disinfecting bottles and mixing the formula. Careful hygiene and correct measuring is vital to ensure the safety of formula-feeding. It is best for parents who wish to feed this way to learn to do so properly.

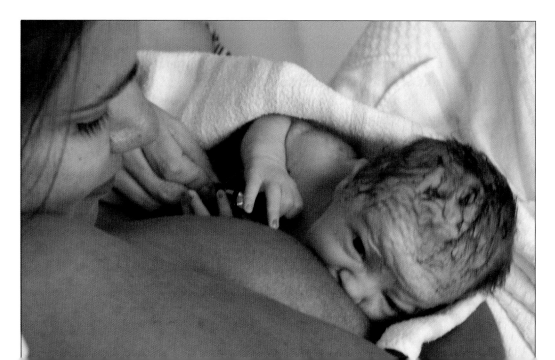

Many women have little or no choice of hospital. Some live in communities where there is only one facility and others are 'zoned' into public maternity service areas. You may not have the luxury of opting for a Baby Friendly hospital. Don't be too concerned. Even if your hospital is not accredited as Baby Friendly, you are likely to have a similar level of care to help you get breastfeeding started. Most will have lactation consultants on staff or on-call. They may also have a lactation day-stay unit so that you can come back if you have problems once you go home.

The average length of hospital stay after a baby is born is 48 hours. Some women are able to go home after 6 hours if that's what they wish and both they and their babies are well. If you've had a caesarean delivery, or you are unwell after a difficult birth, you will usually have an extra couple of days in hospital. This policy suits many women. After all, pregnancy and childbirth are not illnesses. We all usually feel more comfortable at home and are well enough to manage.

Most hospitals will offer an extended postnatal care visit from a midwife the day after you go home, to check how you're going. There are child health services in all states to provide support after the birth of your baby. The early days are a learning experience for both you and your baby. Your milk supply takes quite a few days to become established. Leaving hospital before then means that there may be no-one close at hand to offer skilled help. Make sure you are aware of the support services available to you in case you need them.

A breastfeeding mentor

Having a breastfeeding mentor, someone to call on who can help and support you as you and your baby learn to breastfeed, can be invaluable. Ideally, this would be someone who has successfully breastfed (that doesn't mean that she never had problems), who understands what you are going through.

When mothers look back on their early weeks at home with their babies, many say that they wish they had made personal contact with a breastfeeding support group before their baby's birth. That way, they could have called on someone they already knew and with whom they felt comfortable.

You can find the details of the local ABA group in your area on the ABA website or by contacting ABA. Local group activities aim to give mothers the opportunity to share their breastfeeding and parenting experiences in a relaxed, baby-friendly setting.

Another way of connecting with other breastfeeding women is to join ABA's internet forum where thousands of mothers chat with each other about many and varied issues related to breastfeeding. Go to: *breastfeeding.asn.au>services>forum*.

Health professionals involved in the care of new mothers

Doctors

Research shows that a woman's breastfeeding can be influenced, either positively or negatively, by her doctor's attitudes. Many Australian doctors receive little education about breastfeeding. It's worth the effort to find a doctor who is positive about breastfeeding and who has taken the time to learn how breastfeeding works. That way, you are more likely to get good advice.

Midwives

The health professionals you will see most of during your labour and hospital stay will be midwives. These are nurses with additional training in pregnancy, childbirth and breastfeeding. A midwife looks after the mother medically during and after the birth (and sometimes during pregnancy) and usually helps her to begin breastfeeding. They are very familiar with the normal course of early breastfeeding. If a mother experiences problems, they may recommend she see a lactation consultant.

Child health nurses

Child health nurses are registered nurses with tertiary qualifications in midwifery and maternal and child health. Some have additional training in lactation.

There will be a series of regular checks for your baby as he develops or you can phone if you have concerns. Some centres have drop-in sessions where you can see the nurse for about 15 minutes. When more specialised assistance is needed, child health nurses can make referrals to other health professionals or services.

As well as individual consultations, many centres run group sessions for new mothers with babies of a similar age. These give you the chance to meet other new mums in your area. An ABA group differs from these groups in that they are ongoing. Some ABA meetings discuss a breastfeeding or baby-related topic chosen by the group, while others are purely social gatherings. There are babies and toddlers of all ages so you can talk to mums with babies older than yours. A trained volunteer breastfeeding counsellor is almost always present at these meetings and can answer your questions.

Lactation consultants

Lactation consultants offer support and specialist assistance to mothers who wish to succeed at breastfeeding, or who have problems that have not been resolved by other health professionals. Their job is to get breastfeeding off to a good start and to solve any problems that might arise. You may be able to access a lactation consultant through the post-discharge programs offered by many birthing facilities or through a breastfeeding clinic. You might find that your child health nurse, or your GP, is also a lactation consultant. Outside of the hospital and infant health system, lactation consultants in private practice see mothers on a fee-for-service basis.

An International Board Certified Lactation Consultant (IBCLC) has passed a fully-accredited examination set by the International Board of Lactation Consultant Examiners (IBLCE). The IBCLC certification is recognised as the gold standard for health professionals working with breastfeeding women in Australia and overseas. To find a lactation consultant in your area, see their website: *lcanz.org.* You can also phone ABA's Head Office on 03 9885 0855, or the national Breastfeeding Helpline on 1800 686 268 for this information.

Your partner

More than anyone and anything else, the most vital source of support will be your partner. Indeed, some studies conducted on the role of fathers have shown that their attitude is the most influential factor in whether a woman breastfeeds — more important than doctors, lactation consultants or nurses.

This is why it is important for your partner to be as well informed as you are about breastfeeding. Encourage him (or her) to read this book and any other material you receive. Share your discoveries and feelings about breastfeeding.

Your partner can be an invaluable support at the time of your baby's birth, especially if you need more medical intervention than expected. In this situation, you may be too exhausted to be assertive about breastfeeding your baby as soon as possible after birth. Your partner or support people can step in, if necessary, to ensure that your wishes are respected. They can take charge of nappy changing, burping and soothing an unsettled baby. They can also make sure you have a drink and a snack on hand during feeds. Once you're home again, they can do all of these things plus bathing your baby and taking him for walks either in the pram or a baby sling. Sharing essential tasks like this will allow you to focus on breastfeeding. You can also share routine jobs like cooking, washing and cleaning. Life with a new baby is a team effort.

Maternity bras

'Maternity bra' and 'nursing bra' are the same thing — bras designed for pregnant women as well as breastfeeding. There are so many different styles of maternity or nursing bra available that it can be confusing deciding which one to buy.

Is a maternity bra essential?

Whether or not you wear a bra during pregnancy or breastfeeding is a personal choice. However, the stretching of breast tissues while you are pregnant can contribute to sagging breasts. Wearing a supportive bra may reduce the risk of this happening. Women with larger breasts generally feel more comfortable wearing a bra.

When should I buy a maternity bra?

The right time to be fitted for a maternity bra varies from woman to woman. The breasts begin to prepare for lactation quite early in pregnancy and some women will outgrow their usual bra size earlier than others. Generally speaking, most breast changes have occurred by around 4 months (16 weeks gestation). This is a good time to be fitted for a maternity bra, if you haven't needed to earlier.

How will I know which bra to buy?

A correctly fitted bra gives you comfort and support, so it is a good idea to be professionally fitted. This is a free service. You will be fitted for the size you are at the time, as maternity bras are designed to cope with the changes to your breasts that come with pregnancy and birth. It is not necessary to buy a bra you will grow into.

Indeed too big can be as bad as too small! When trying on different styles of bras, remember to open and close the bra cup, as some are easier to manage than others. Look for bras where the whole cup drops away, as 'trapdoor' styles can put pressure on a full breast. Centre front and shoulder clasp styles are available. Many mothers prefer styles that are easy to manage with one hand, particularly when they are away from home. These days, maternity bras come in a range of fashionable styles and colours.

Can I wear an underwire bra?
Inflexible underwire bras are not recommended during pregnancy or lactation because of your changing breast shape. During breastfeeding, your breasts may increase and decrease in size during the day, as milk is produced and removed. Retained fluid in late pregnancy can also cause them to swell. Although the change in size may only be slight, a rigid underwire may put pressure on the breast when it is fuller. This can lead to blocked milk ducts or mastitis. However, nursing bras are now available with a flexible plastic support, similar to an underwire, designed to flex and change position with your changing shape. They are less likely to cause problems.

Should I wear a bra to bed?
Some women feel they need the support of a bra in bed or something to hold nursing pads in place; others find it uncomfortable. You can buy special sleep bras or wear a 'singlet' top or other soft cup bra in the correct size.

Breast pumps

Many women (mistakenly) think that a breast pump is essential for successful breastfeeding. However, it's something you can put off buying until you know how often you will be using the pump, or indeed, whether you even need one at all.

Each breast pump is designed for a specific level of usage. Chapter 17 has more details about the use of breast pumps.

CHAPTER 4

How breastfeeding works

Breasts are made for breastfeeding

Breast surgery and breastfeeding

Nipples and breastfeeding

How breasts make milk

Supply and demand

What's in a breastfeed?

Believing in yourself

From the time our breasts first appear, most women spend a lot of time worrying about their size and shape. Few of us think our breasts are perfect. In a culture where appearance is so important, a woman's attitude to her breasts can influence her feelings of femininity, self-esteem and even her posture. Whatever their size or shape, no-one ever tells us that our breasts are nothing short of miraculous.

Regardless of how you felt about your breasts before pregnancy, the actual experience of breastfeeding and seeing your baby growing on your milk alone can give you new insight into your body and its amazing abilities.

Breasts are made for breastfeeding

Breastfeeding is an instinctive natural function. However, in our culture, doing what comes naturally is not always easy. Women have lost confidence in their body's ability to carry, birth and breastfeed their babies. Breastfeeding does not require any special equipment and costs nothing but time and patience, knowledge and support.

How your breasts get ready to breastfeed
When you are pregnant, the focus is on your growing belly. Although the changes to your breasts may be less obvious to others, they are just as dramatic. The breasts of a woman who has borne a child, whether or not she breastfeeds, are different from those of a woman who has never been pregnant.

You may notice:
- tender breasts
- tingling or sore nipples (some women's breasts become so sensitive that touching them is painful)
- the areola (area of skin around the nipple) gets larger and may become darker
- blood vessels are more visible
- the 'lumps' on your areola (called Montgomery's glands) become more obvious
- that in the last trimester of your pregnancy, you may be able to express some drops of liquid (called colostrum) or your nipples may leak
- your breasts increase in size because of the new glandular tissue in the breast.

All of these changes prepare your body for breastfeeding your baby. Whether she is born at term or is premature, your breasts will produce milk.

How your breasts change after your baby is born
For the first day or so after the birth, your breasts will be making the 'power food',

colostrum. As your milk 'comes in', your breasts usually start to feel very full and tight. Squeezing the areola can result in sprays of milk. While your baby is feeding from one breast, milk may leak from the other. It is easy to think that your breasts are full of milk. However, only part of this initial fullness is breastmilk. The rest is extra blood and tissue fluid that build up in your breasts as they start full production.

As your breasts settle down, they adjust the amount of milk they are making in response to the amount of milk your baby is drinking. You may find that they no longer look or feel as 'full'. This does not mean that you are losing your milk, or that your breasts are not making enough. It means that your body has fine-tuned the delicate balance between supply and demand. As you continue to breastfeed, your breasts may not be much bigger than they were before your pregnancy. They may not feel full at all, unless you miss a feed.

The structure of the breast

Your breasts are made up of glandular tissue, supporting connective tissue and protective fatty tissue. The size of the breast depends on the amount of fatty tissue, which in turn largely depends on genetics. So your mother and grandmother influence the size of your breasts — but not your ability to breastfeed. The milk is produced in the glandular tissue. The shape and size of your breasts have very little bearing on this. A big-breasted woman may have a small amount of glandular tissue and a large amount of protective fatty tissue, while a small-breasted woman may have the reverse. Women with a small amount of glandular tissue are still able to breastfeed successfully.

While their size can vary enormously, all breasts have the same basic structure. Each breast has about nine lobes of milk-making glandular tissue. The lobes are made

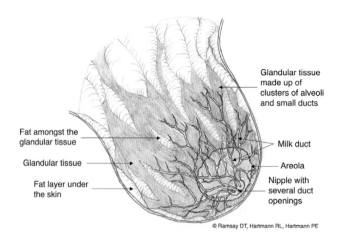

Fat amongst the glandular tissue

Glandular tissue made up of clusters of alveoli and small ducts

Glandular tissue

Milk duct

Fat layer under the skin

Areola

Nipple with several duct openings

© Ramsay DT, Hartmann RL, Hartmann PE

up of clusters of alveoli, which contain the cells where breastmilk is produced. Special channels, called ducts, carry the milk towards the nipple. The milk then flows out through tiny openings in the nipple.

The size and colour of the areola varies between women. The Montgomery's glands provide natural lubrication which also helps prevent bacteria growing on the nipples.

It is rare for a woman not to be able to breastfeed. There is no such thing as having the 'wrong' type of breasts, or the 'wrong' nipples.

Breast surgery and breastfeeding

Breast cancer is the most commonly diagnosed cancer in women of reproductive age and treatment may involve breast surgery. Other women may have had surgery as part of treatment for the removal of a breast abscess or to change the shape or size of their breasts.

If you have had breast surgery before becoming pregnant, no-one will be able to tell you for sure whether you will be able to breastfeed. Each surgery and each breast is different, so each woman's chance of success will be different. Only by trying to breastfeed will you know whether it will work for you.

If the essential elements of ducts, nipple and areola, glandular tissue and nerves are damaged, then breastfeeding will be more difficult. If you told your doctors prior to your surgery that you wanted to breastfeed in the future, they will have tried to minimise such damage during the operation. Many surgeons will do this anyway whenever they operate on women of child-bearing age. Being able to express colostrum before your baby is born is a good sign. Even when you can't, you may still be able to breastfeed. The right advice and support has enabled many women with breast implants, or a breast reduction, to breastfeed from one or both breasts.

Nipples and breastfeeding

As you would imagine, your nipples play an important part in breastfeeding. They have smooth muscle that enables them to become erect in response to stimulation. When they are not erect, nipples usually look slightly flat. When you are in contact with your baby, when you are cold, or when you are sexually aroused, they stand out. When your baby suckles, your nipple extends to form a teat, which is up to three times its original length. Each nipple contains anything from 4 to 18 (the average being 9) openings, or nipple pores.

'Breast' feeding, not nipple feeding
The type of sucking action a baby uses to 'milk' the breast is very different from the action she would use to suck milk from a straw or from a bottle teat.

When your baby breastfeeds, she needs to draw the nipple as well as a good mouthful of breast into her mouth. Your nipple will stretch far back into her mouth almost to the junction between the hard and soft palate. Her tongue forms a trough around the nipple, so that the action of her tongue and jaw compresses the breast tissue. Rhythmical tongue movements create suction to express milk into the back of her mouth.

If your nipple is not drawn to the back of your baby's mouth, it can get squashed between her tongue and hard palate. This causes pain.

Pierced nipples
If you have had your nipples pierced you should still be able to breastfeed. If you have a piercing, you'll have had it before you became pregnant, so it should be completely healed. (Pregnant women shouldn't have piercings or tattoos and breastfeeding mothers should wait until after they have weaned.) It's advisable to remove the jewellery before each feed, but you might find that constantly removing and reinserting

it makes tender nipples become quite sore. If you wish to keep the jewellery in place, you should think about whether it could damage your baby's mouth or even come off.

Inverted nipples

Some women's nipples become erect easily. Others have to be coaxed out and some seem to be flat or even go in instead of out. Nipples that go in rather than out are known as inverted nipples. If you have nipples like this, you can still breastfeed. However, you may need a little extra help to get breastfeeding started. Your breasts and nipples can change dramatically during your pregnancy. You may find that nature does her job and your 'introverted' nipples gradually become more 'extroverted' as your breasts grow.

How breasts make milk

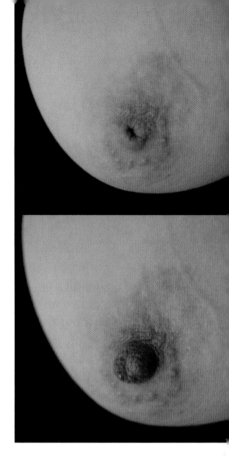

Some 'inverted' nipples can be coaxed out

Understanding how your breasts make milk can help you avoid or overcome some of the problems that have come to be associated with breastfeeding.

Firstly, while you don't need large breasts to breastfeed, you do need a baby with a good appetite. A baby who feeds well and often ensures you have a good milk supply. Fortunately, almost all babies are born with the instinct to suck (the sucking reflex) and are keen to get started.

When your baby attaches to the breast and begins to feed, nerve impulses are carried to your brain, causing the release of hormones. One (prolactin) stimulates the milk-producing glands in the breast, while another (oxytocin) causes the ejection of milk. It also lowers your blood pressure, heart rate and anxiety levels while, at the same time, increasing insulin and blood glucose levels, as well as your pain threshold. For many women, the act of breastfeeding is very calming.

At the start of a feed, your baby's initial rapid sucking stimulates nerve endings in the skin covering the nipple. This triggers the release of the milk stored in the glandular tissues of the breast. This release is commonly called the let-down reflex (or the milk-ejection reflex). The let-down reflex works something like a valve or tap. It is this reflex that makes your milk available to your baby.

The let-down reflex — a physical action and a conditioned response
When your milk lets down, the cells surrounding the alveoli contract and squeeze out the milk, forcing it down the now expanded ducts towards the nipple. This may take anything from an instant to a couple of minutes. You may notice:
- a tingling sensation in your breasts
- a sudden feeling of fullness
- in the early days, especially if this is not your first baby, your uterus contracting (this is known as 'after-pains' and may be nearly as strong as the contractions you experienced early in your labour)
- milk dripping from the other breast as you breastfeed.

About 30% of women don't notice any of these signs, but all can see a change in their baby's sucking rhythm, from rapid little sucks to a slower and stronger suck-and-swallow action, as the milk starts to flow.

The let-down reflex occurs, on average, two or three times during each feed, as the oxytocin is released in a pulsing manner throughout the feed. Most mothers will only notice the first let-down (if they notice it at all). Unless you're experiencing a problem with your milk supply, your let-down reflex is something you don't have to think about — it will just happen.

Just as your mouth may begin to water when you are hungry and smell something delicious cooking, the sight or sound of your baby, or even just thinking about her, may trigger your let-down reflex. It can also happen if you stimulate the breast and nipple area with your fingers. People often say that your let-down may not work as well if you are very anxious, extremely tired, upset or in pain. The truth is that breastfeeding is a powerful process. With support and encouragement, mothers cope with many different stresses and still breastfeed successfully.

Supply and demand

The principle of supply and demand, or demand equals supply, is probably the most important thing to know about breastfeeding. How much milk your breasts make depends on how often your baby breastfeeds and how much milk she takes. It is the removal of the milk that causes more milk to be made.

A special type of peptide (a very small protein) found in breastmilk, regulates how much milk is made. As your breasts fill up with milk, the amount of this peptide builds up in your glandular tissue. This gives your breasts the message that they have made nearly enough milk and should slow down production. The more milk that is removed, either when your baby feeds or when you express your milk, the lower the level of the peptide. This tells your breasts to make more milk. Each breast operates independently and produces different amounts of milk.

There is a big variation between mothers in the amount of milk they produce each day. This is because there is a big variation in how much milk babies take. Australian studies show a range of 500–1200 mL per day, the average being 800 mL. Once your milk supply is established by around the first month after birth, the volume produced remains fairly constant until about 6 months.

For the vast majority of mothers, it is easy to make sure their baby gets enough breastmilk. Just follow your baby's feeding cues and don't limit her time at the breast: that's all you have to do.

Your breasts are never actually empty. Babies stop feeding when they have had enough, while at the same time, your breasts are already at work making more milk. Studies that have measured the amount of milk a baby takes show that about 65% of the available milk is used at each feed. Whatever your baby drinks is automatically replaced, producing a constant supply, perfectly matched to her need, whenever she needs it.

When my brain made sense of breastfeeding, it seemed that my breasts and I did too! Most of the hiccups I encountered may have been overcome or avoided with just a little knowledge. If you are planning to breastfeed, asking lots of questions and listening to others' experiences will set you on the road to success.

What's in a breastfeed?

A breastfeed is like a long warm drink and a hot meal, all in one package. Scientists have already identified many hundreds of ingredients in breastmilk (and the list continues to grow). If breastmilk was packaged in a can, we'd be hard pressed to find space on the label to list them all.

Every mother's breastmilk is uniquely programmed to meet the particular needs of her own baby. For example, the milk of mothers of premature babies differs from that of mothers of full-term babies. If she and her baby are exposed to bacteria or viruses, the antibodies she makes quickly enter her breastmilk to protect her baby.

The first milk that your breasts produce is called colostrum. It is high in immuno-globulins (or antibodies, which boost your baby's resistance to infection); lactoferrin (which protects against infection and helps the absorption of iron); chloride and sodium (salt); and low in lactose (milk sugar) and fat. Nature has designed it so that your baby's immature kidneys do not have to work too hard. At birth, a baby's stomach is about the size of a marble and is not yet stretchy. The amount of colostrum a baby receives at each feed is small but highly concentrated. It is designed that way so babies can gradually ease into taking their food by mouth and slowly stretch out their stomach.

There is a big increase in volume once your milk comes in. Mature breastmilk has higher concentrations of lactose and fat than colostrum. Its anti-infective properties remain the same, but are diluted by the increased volume of milk. You will continue to make mature breastmilk for as long as your baby keeps breastfeeding. You can feel confident that the overall protective levels remain constant and that breastmilk keeps its nutritional value after many months or even years of breastfeeding.

The fat composition of milk changes as each feed progresses. Milk at the end of a feed has a higher fat content than at the start. It is important to allow your baby to set the pace of feeds, rather than timing them by the clock. A baby who is allowed to feed until she is ready to come off the breast herself receives the right balance of both fats and other nutrients. If you take her off after only a few minutes, particularly in the early days when she may not be as efficient at milking the breast, she will only receive the warm drink. This can result in the wrong balance of nutrients, which in turn may cause too much or too little milk. Either of these can result in a very unhappy baby. It is best to allow the baby to feed on each side for as long as she wants. As a guide, most babies will spend about 30 minutes on each side in the early days. This time will get shorter as she gets older.

If you keep breastfeeding past your baby's first year, your breastmilk remains an important part of her diet. It will continue to provide vital protection from infection as she begins to have more contact with other adults and children.

During weaning, your milk will start to resemble colostrum again, with a greater proportion of sodium, protein and anti-infective factors and less lactose. This is nature's way of giving your baby a final protective boost.

What breastmilk looks like

We are so used to seeing homogenised and pasteurised cows' milk, which is consistently white, that the appearance of breastmilk can come as quite a surprise.

Colostrum is a thick, yellowish fluid. After the first couple of days and, for the next week or so, your breasts will produce a mixture of both colostrum and mature milk, making it look creamier than straight, mature breastmilk. If it has to be compared to the milk we are most familiar with, mature breastmilk looks a little like skim milk, but is more pearl-like in colour and translucent. It may sometimes look a little bluish.

The fuller your breasts, the bluer your breastmilk will look. The emptier your breasts, the creamier your milk will look. Its fat content varies with the time of day and the number of feeds your baby has had over that day.

Believing in yourself

Successful breastfeeding is something of a confidence trick. As well as focusing on how breastfeeding works, it's useful to remember that our feelings and the support we have from friends and family can also influence our breastfeeding outcomes. Focus on the following tips to help you reach your breastfeeding goals:

- Be confident that your body can nourish your baby through breastfeeding, just as it did through pregnancy. Your body can produce milk that is good for your baby, in quantities enough to meet all her nutritional needs.
- Believe that you know your baby better than anyone else and that your own needs are also important. Trust your decisions about how to feed her and what is best for you both.
- Try to keep calm when faced with problems. Clear thinking usually helps you work out how to solve them.
- Communicate clearly. Tell people what you and your baby need and make sure

you are heard and responded to.

- Have confidence in yourself. Take control and ask for help when needed from your partner, family and support services.
- Look after yourself. You need emotional and physical energy to get through the early, learning stage of breastfeeding or any problems that may arise.
- Observe your baby closely so that you learn the meaning of her behaviours and the noises she makes. This will make it easier for you to respond to her and meet her needs.
- Learn to deal with the unknown — to accept that you won't always know what is happening, or when or how things might change. You won't always know exactly what your baby wants, but you can rely on the signs that tell you that she is getting enough breastmilk.

Breastfeeding was going pretty well by the time I left hospital. However, I think I never truly felt comfortable with my breastfeeding ability at the start, despite having a happy baby with all the correct 'healthy' signs (weight gains, wet nappies etc). I do not think I was ever really confident that she was doing well on my breastmilk, as I could not see how much she had taken each feed. However, knowing about the number of wet nappies in 24 hours, the fact she was thriving and the encouragement from my ABA group kept me going.

CHAPTER 5

How to breastfeed

Baby-led attachment

Mother-assisted attachment

Breastfeeding while lying down

Positioning and attachment checklist

As you fumble your way through those first breastfeeds, holding your breath in nervous concentration and excitement, it can be hard to imagine that you'll soon be so confident that you will be breastfeeding without even thinking about how to do it.

You'll read and hear a lot about 'positioning and attachment' as you learn more about breastfeeding. Positioning is how you hold your baby at your breast and position him to ensure that he can attach (or latch on) to your breast properly, feed effectively and get as much of the available breastmilk as he needs. There are two main ways to attach your baby. These are suggestions only. There is no right or wrong.

The important things are that breastfeeding is pain-free, you and your baby are comfortable and he is getting enough milk.

Baby-led attachment — a step-by-step guide

Babies are hardwired to seek out their mother's breast and, if left to their own devices, are able to attach themselves and start to feed. 'Baby-led attachment' is a term used to describe this process. Your own instincts and your natural anxiety are probably telling you to bring your baby to your breast and put your nipple into his mouth for him. But if you can allow your baby to take charge, you'll be amazed at what happens. Baby-led attachment offers your baby the most natural introduction to breastfeeding.

1. Sit comfortably

You can do this in bed with pillows behind you and one under your knees, or on a chair with your feet on a low stool or cushion. If you're in a hospital bed, which will probably be very narrow and quite high, you may feel more secure if you put the sides up. You need to be leaning back rather than sitting upright. Make sure you are well-supported and comfortable, as you may be in that position for a while. Speak to your medical adviser if pain is making it difficult for you to relax.

2. Baby needs to be calm and alert

Humans learn best when they are calm. Your baby's instincts will lead him to move to the breast and suckle. However, it is the flow of milk he then receives that teaches him that this is where milk comes from. Baby-led attachment works best if the baby is a little bit hungry. But if he is frantic for a feed, stressed, crying or too sleepy, he will not be able to follow his instincts. If he is upset, calm him by gentle rocking and cuddling. Talk to your baby, make eye contact and hold him skin-to-skin. Letting him suck on your clean finger can also help to calm him.

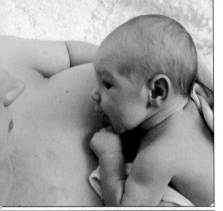
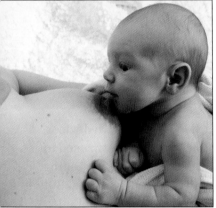

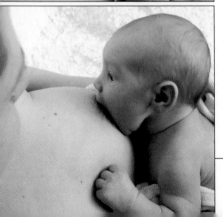

3. Have skin-to-skin contact with your baby

This is a very important part of the process, so you may find it helps to remove your top and bra. If you need your top on for warmth, leave it completely open at the front. It's best to take your baby's clothes off too, except for his nappy. Make sure the room is warm enough to be comfortable for you both. You can always pull up a sheet/blanket/doona once he is attached. In these early days, keeping your baby skin-to-skin on your chest as much as possible will encourage him to feed when he is ready.

4. Hold your baby against your body

Hold your baby upright on your chest, between your breasts. As you are leaning back, gravity will help keep your bodies in close contact.

5. Let your baby follow his instincts

As your baby starts to follow his instincts, he may start to 'bob' his head against your chest. Support his body but allow him to move freely. He will start to slide, crawl, fall or even throw himself towards one of your breasts.

6. Support your baby

As he starts to move towards one breast, it may help to move his bottom across your body. However, keep him in a semi-vertical position, with his feet supported by your thigh. You may also need to move your hand and wrist to support his back and shoulders. Do not hold his head. Supporting your baby's upper body makes him stable enough to be able to control his head movements as he attaches.

7. Allow your baby to attach to your breast

Now that your baby's head is near your nipple, he may nuzzle your breast for a little while. That's fine. As long as he is still calm, let him find his own way. When he is ready he will dig his chin into your breast, reach up with an open mouth and attach to the breast. You may find it helps to pull your baby's bottom closer to your body, or to give even more firm support to his back and shoulders at this time. This will help him to dig his chin in, keep his nose free of the breast and get a good mouthful of breast. If he loses contact with your breast, the whole process may stop. He may continue once in contact again. If he doesn't, move him back to a more upright position between your breasts and start again.

Mother-assisted attachment — a step-by-step guide

This is a more structured approach to positioning and attachment. A baby who has already made a good start with baby-led attachment should transfer easily to this method when you are both ready. In circumstances when baby-led attachment is not possible, this is how most mothers begin to learn to breastfeed.

1. Make yourself comfortable
You can feed your baby while sitting or lying down, whichever feels right for you. If you prefer to lie down, you might find it more comfortable to use a couple of extra pillows to tuck under your shoulder or behind your back. Lie on your side, with your body slightly curved so that your baby can snuggle in next to you. If you're sitting up, you can use pillows to support your back. A pillow on your lap may make it easier for you to bring your baby's nose level with your nipple (don't bring him up too high though).

2. Make it easier for you and your baby to get closer
Make sure your clothes (including your bra) don't restrict your baby's

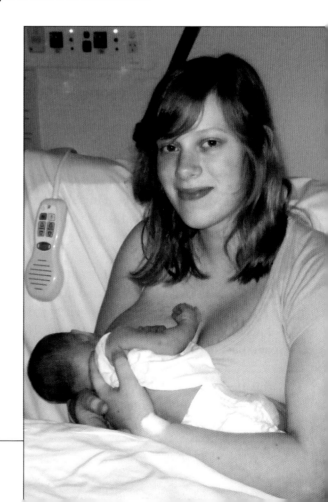

close contact with your breast, or your view of his attachment. Clothes that unbutton to the waist make it easier. You may even like to remove your top while you are learning to breastfeed, rather than tuck it under your chin. The last thing you want is to have clothes getting in the way when you're concentrating on trying to attach your baby to your breast.

> **Avoid wrapping your baby snugly to keep his hands out of the way as this may not allow him to get close enough to attach comfortably. A baby's natural instinct is to have his hands near his head and on his mother's chest, not held by his sides.**

3. Position your baby to attach to your breast
Turn your baby onto his side, his nose level with your nipple. Hold him behind his shoulders and neck (not his head) or rest his head on your forearm close to but not in the crook of your elbow. Pull your baby in close to you, aligning his body at a slight angle to you, with his chin closer to your breast than his nose.

Your baby's whole body should be turned towards you so that his hips, tummy and chest are against you. Make sure that his mouth and nose are directly opposite your nipple.

4. Encourage your baby
Gently brush your baby's mouth with your nipple and the underside of your areola. Wait for him to instinctively nuzzle and open his mouth wide to gape for your breast. His natural rooting reflex will help him find the nipple. Until you become more confident, you may find it helps to support the breast. Avoid moving or lifting your breast or chasing his mouth with your nipple. Try to keep your nipple in its natural position (where it would be if unsupported by your hand). A rolled up towel under the breast may help to lift the breast so that you can see the nipple, but still not change the natural position of your breast or nipple.

5. Bring your baby to your breast
When his mouth is wide open and his tongue is well forward over his bottom gum, you can bring your baby quickly but gently to your breast. Aim the nipple towards the roof of his mouth, guiding it over his tongue. He needs to get not only the nipple but also a good part of the breast into his mouth.

> **It is important that the baby takes in as much of the nipple and areola as possible, with the greatest part being on the chin side of the nipple.**

Breastfeeding while lying down — a step-by-step guide

It will come as no surprise to you that mothers (particularly new mothers) get tired — sometimes very tired. There will be times when you'll feel that you simply have to lie down before you drop. Most mothers find breastfeeding in bed very comfortable once they're confident that their babies are attaching well. Most babies love the experience.

1. Place your baby on his back in the middle of a large bed.
2. Lie on your side, next to your baby with your head on a pillow (make sure the pillow is not near your baby's head). You can also put a pillow between your legs and one up against your back if these help make you more comfortable.
3. Slide your baby so that his nose is in line with your nipple and your arm is above his head (don't rest his head on your arm). Keeping your arm clear of his head will stop your body heat from making his head sweaty.
4. Roll your baby onto his side toward you and pull his hips up close to your hips, letting his nose just gently make contact with your nipple. If he is very tiny and cannot stay in this position by himself, you could put a corner of a pillow up against his bottom (not near his head).
5. Your baby can then stretch up slightly with a wide gape and attach. If you need to help your baby attach, you can use the arm that is not resting on the bed to shape your breast and guide the nipple into the baby's mouth. Some babies are good at attaching and you can let them latch on by themselves. Older babies can also usually find their own way.
6. When the time comes for the second side, some mothers lean over a bit further and feed from the top breast. Others prefer to roll over and move the baby to their other side.

When you feel so sure of yourself that you could almost breastfeed swinging from a chandelier, it will be because you have the basic technique down pat.

Positioning and attachment checklist

When your baby is well positioned and attached:

✓ His mouth will be right over the nipple and well onto the areola.

✓ His tongue will be well forward, cupping the nipple and areola.

✓ He will have more of the chin-side of the areola in his mouth than the side nearest to his nose.

✓ His top and bottom lips will be turned out (flanged) over the breast (the lower lip more so than the top lip).

✓ His chin will be pressed against the breast.

✓ His head will be tipped back a little.

✓ His nose will be clear so that he can breathe easily. You shouldn't need to hold your breast away from his nose. Doing this may pull the nipple from his mouth or even block the milk ducts below your finger. If his nose is pushing into your breast, try moving his body and legs closer to you. This will bring his chin further towards the breast and free his nostrils naturally.

✓ He will be close enough to you so that he doesn't have to strain to hold on to the breast.

✓ Your breasts won't feel painful beyond the initial stretching of your nipple.

NOTE: If breastfeeding hurts, place a clean finger in your baby's mouth at the corner to break the suction, remove your nipple from his mouth and start again.

CHAPTER 6

How often, for how long and how much?

How often should my baby breastfeed?

How long should each breastfeed last?

How can I tell if I have enough milk?

What is the 'normal' growth rate
for babies?

Every new mother feels uncertain about whether she is managing as well as other mothers. We all want to do everything right and provide the best possible care for our new babies. The three most common questions that new breastfeeding mothers ask are:

'How often should I breastfeed my baby?'
'How long should a breastfeed last?'
'How can I tell if I have enough milk?'

Once you know the answers to these three questions, you'll have a grasp of the basics of successful breastfeeding.

How often should my baby breastfeed?

'You're not feeding again, are you?' You may often hear comments like this from people who are not used to breastfed babies. The common belief that babies should feed every 4 hours is an obstacle to breastfeeding that has been almost impossible to overcome. Yet there is no evidence that supports this belief. In fact, a 4-hour gap between breastfeeds is actually a very long time, particularly in the first few months.

> **Breastfeeding 6 times in 24 hours is usually not enough to build a good milk supply. It is often a recipe for a hungry and unsettled baby and can result in unplanned early weaning.**

You may be told that feeding every 2 hours, or topping up after 20 minutes or an hour, will make your baby sick, fat, spoiled or, worse still, that is a sign that your milk is not 'good enough'. Fortunately none of this is true.

You may also like to remind yourself, and others, that during the day few adults go 4 hours without having something to eat and/or drink. Breastmilk is not only food and a drink, but also comfort and security for your baby.

What is true is that:

- **Little babies feed very often.** After the first day, babies need to breastfeed at least 8 times in every 24 hours. Research (and experience) has shown that, in their first couple of months, babies feed between 8 and 17 times in a day. The average is 11 times.
- **Your milk is extremely well absorbed by your baby.** Unlike infant formula, it will not take long to digest.

- **A baby's stomach is very tiny** (about the size of her clenched fist) so it doesn't take much to fill it.
- **Babies show signs of being ready to feed** well before they start to cry. Crying is a late sign of hunger and you don't have to wait for her to cry before offering her a breastfeed. She is more likely to feed well if she is not exhausted and distressed by crying before the feed starts.

Early signs of infant hunger are:
- sucking movements and sounds
- hand-to-mouth movements
- rapid eye movements
- restlessness
- soft cooing or sighing sounds
- turning her head from side to side searching for the breast
- opening her mouth
- sucking her hands.

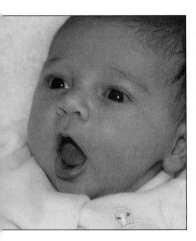 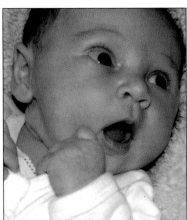 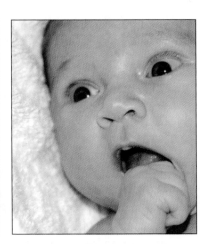

Few babies younger than about 3 months sleep for long periods between feeds. If they do, they will make up for it by having unsettled periods when they need more frequent feeding.

- Between 4–9 weeks almost all babies feed during the night and from 9–26 weeks at least 60% of babies are still doing so.

- A baby who sleeps for long periods may need to be woken. Some may appear very sleepy and undemanding. They consistently sleep for several hours and have little active awake time. A good rule of thumb is to make sure a sleepy baby breastfeeds at least 3-hourly during the day and at least once during the night.
- Colicky babies can be miserable and want to feed constantly. They may actually be getting too much milk, too fast and have a tummy ache. If your baby is like this, read Chapter 15. A breastfeeding counsellor can give you ideas to help.

How long should each breastfeed last?

Every baby is different. Some babies like to linger over dinner, while others like to eat and run, so to speak. The baby is usually the best judge of how often and for how long she needs to feed. She has not read books that suggest strict schedules. Imagine how you would feel if someone told you when and for how long you could eat. Some people call this baby-led feeding routine 'demand-feeding'. Experienced mothers know that it is really feeding according to the baby's need.

Overall length of a feed
There is no need to restrict the length of feeds. You will find that the time taken to breastfeed your baby varies from feed to feed. In each 24-hour period some feeds will be only 5–10 minutes long. Others may be 30 minutes or longer, particularly when she feeds to sleep slowly and contentedly. However, spending a very long time at the breast, more than an hour, may be a sign that a baby is not getting enough milk to satisfy her. A chat with a breastfeeding counsellor may help you understand the issues involved.

Length of feed from each breast
Let your baby feed from one breast until she stops actively feeding. She will either let go of the nipple or fall asleep. Cuddle your baby and give her a chance to bring up any wind she may have. Then, if she is still awake and interested, offer the second breast, again for as long she wants.

One breast or both?
Some babies are content to feed from only one side each time in the early weeks. Over time they will gradually start to feed from both breasts most times. During the time you are feeding from only one breast, start each feed on the side your baby didn't have last time. This way, each breast receives the same amount of stimulation. This prevents engorgement and ensures you maintain your supply.

Signs of milk transfer

It helps to be able to recognise when your baby is actively feeding and receiving the milk she needs. Babies who are taking milk well from the breast have a rhythmic suck/swallow/breathe pattern. There are no rules about how many sucks or breaths there are between each swallow. The number changes during a feed. You should be able to hear her swallow and see her relax as the feed progresses.

As well as hearing your baby swallowing, there are other signs that you are making milk. Usually milk volume increases by about day 3 after the birth. Your breasts will gradually feel fuller over the time between feeds. Milk may drip from the second breast while your baby is feeding from the first. At the end of a feed your breasts may feel less full (although if your breasts are very full and tight, you may not notice much of a difference). These breast changes usually become less noticeable as your baby gets older and your breasts get used to producing the amount of milk she needs.

How can I tell if I have enough milk?

It is common for mothers who weaned their babies early to say that they weaned because they were worried they didn't have enough milk. However, nearly all mothers are able to make enough breastmilk for their babies.

While you can see how much milk a baby takes from a bottle, this is not the case with breastfeeding. Fortunately there are a number of signs, when put together, that tell you that your baby is getting enough milk.

1. Wet nappies

What goes in must come out. After day 5, your baby should have at least 6 very wet cloth nappies in 24 hours, provided no other fluids or solids are being given. If you are using disposable nappies, particularly those containing moisture-absorbing gel, you should expect at least 5 nappies in 24 hours. However, the nappies should feel heavy after use. Over the first 3–4 days, salts of uric acid in your baby's wee may leave a rusty, orange-red stain on the nappy. This is perfectly normal during this time. If you see staining on your baby's nappy later than this, it's usually a sign that she is not getting enough breastmilk.

2. Bowel motions
- **Frequency:** For the first week, she may have a bowel motion at each nappy change. Then over the next 6 weeks or so, you can expect at least 3 poos a day. Having less than one dirty nappy a day in a baby of this age usually means she

needs more breastmilk. As the weeks go by your baby may have fewer soiled nappies. Not all babies are the same, and the number may vary from daily to once or twice a week. It's all normal as long as the stools (poo) are soft and unformed.

- **Colour**: In the first 48 hours, meconium will make your baby's poo look dark and sticky. Over days 3–4, her poo will change to a greenish brown-yellow. From about day 5 it will look like yellow mustard or runny egg or thick pumpkin soup. Normal colour ranges from yellow through to greenish-gold to brown. A green bowel motion is nothing to worry about in an otherwise healthy baby. Stools will turn green when they're exposed to air.
- **Consistency**: They will be mostly liquid, with small curds that look a bit like cottage cheese. You might see just liquid at one nappy change and a thicker consistency at the next. You might wonder whether liquid stools are a sign that your baby has diarrhoea. In fact, diarrhoea in the breastfed baby is rare. A baby who has diarrhoea would have foul-smelling stools that are very frequent, usually green and full of mucus (and even specks of blood).
- **Quantity**: The amount can vary from a stain on the nappy to, 'Run the bath and get the washing machine ready'.
- **Smell**: The poo of a breastfed baby usually has very little odour. In some babies it is quite sweet-smelling. Overall, the smell is not offensive.

3. Skin tone and eyes
Your baby should have a healthy skin colour, bright eyes and good skin and muscle tone. Does she look as though she fits in her skin? If you gently 'pinch' her skin, it should spring back into place.

4. Behaviour
Your baby should be alert and reasonably contented for parts of the day, even if she has some fussy or very unsettled times as well. She will usually wake for night feeds. Very few babies sleep for a lengthy period during the night. Most wake during the night for quite some time. It's worth knowing that 'sleeping through' in young babies is defined as sleeping for 5 hours!

5. Growth and development
There should be some weight gain and growth in length and head circumference. It is important not to get too focused on weight gain. Most babies do not put on a set amount of weight every week, but you should see a gradual gain in weight over each 3–4 week period. However, a baby should show consistent growth over the first year. She should be meeting her developmental milestones.

What is the 'normal' growth rate for babies?

Over the first 12 months of your baby's life, each time you visit the child health centre or your doctor, they will pay quite a bit of attention to your child's growth and development. It can sometimes feel as though you have to pass an exam each time your baby is weighed and measured. We all want our babies to pass the test — to be like other babies.

It's worth knowing a bit more about growth rates and milestones and the tools used to measure your baby's development. This may save you unnecessary worry.

In general, the guidelines are that:
- A baby will lose 5–10% of birth weight in the first week and regain this by 2–3 weeks.
- Birth weight will double by 4 months and triple by 13 months in boys and 15 months in girls.
- Birth length will increase 1.5 times in 12 months.
- Birth head circumference will increase by about 11 cm in 12 months.

However, all babies grow differently. Some adults are naturally petite and so are some babies. Some families are taller. If your baby is having plenty of wet and dirty nappies, appears to be happy and healthy and is meeting developmental milestones, then her size may be due to family factors (genetics).

If you are concerned about your baby's growth, contact your medical adviser for a thorough assessment of your baby's general health and wellbeing.

When is low weight gain a problem?
Individual babies vary a lot and weight is only one factor in the 'whole picture' of a baby's health and development.

Looking at your undressed baby can also give you an idea of how she is growing. Does your baby look healthy? Does she have a good skin colour and muscle tone? Does she look the right weight for her size? Does she look like her skin 'fits'? Wrinkly, loose skin with not enough fat beneath it is a sign that your baby is not gaining enough weight or is losing weight. The 'wasting' of weight loss first appears around a baby's lower abdomen, buttocks and upper thighs, so remove all your baby's clothes, especially the nappy, when checking this.

Make an appointment with your medical adviser who will look at your baby's general health and check that she is meeting her developmental milestones.

What if a baby has been gaining weight well but has now suddenly slowed down?

If your baby has been gaining well, some slow-down is normal. It is very common for exclusively breastfed babies to gain weight more slowly at 3–4 months. The World Health Organization child growth standards, based on healthy breastfed babies, show this. You can find these on ABA's website: *breastfeeding.asn.au> information>common concerns baby*.

If there's a concern about your baby's weight gains and you are worried about your milk supply, ask these questions:

- Could the weighing technique be the problem? Was she weighed on the same scales, in the same clothes? Did her nappy weigh about the same? Was she weighed before or after a feed, before or after a large bowel motion? Have your baby weighed a second time, in case there was a mistake.
- Have there been any changes in your baby's behaviour? For example, has she been taking fewer feeds because she has started sleeping longer at night?
- Have you been trying to feed at set times instead of whenever the baby asks?
- Have you been stressed or unwell? Have you had mastitis?
- Have you just started a new medication such as the contraceptive pill? Could you be pregnant? Both these factors can cause a dip in your supply.
- Has your baby been ill? Even a small cold can disrupt feeding and weight gain for a week or two. Has she recently been immunised?

In most cases where there is a sudden weight change in a baby who has been growing well, it is usually safe to 'wait and see' for a couple of weeks. If you think that your milk supply may have dropped temporarily, offering a couple of extra breastfeeds a day may be enough to solve the problem.

You may wish to talk to your doctor if your baby seems unhappy, or there are other aspects of her growth and health that are worrying you.

Can test weighing tell me how much milk my baby is getting?
Some mothers judge their milk supply by how their breasts feel. This is very unreliable. Your breasts tend to feel softer and less full once your milk supply is established and they get used to doing what they are meant to do.

Sometimes, well-meaning friends or family members or even health professionals may suggest that you express some breastmilk to 'see how much milk you have'. This is not a good idea. How much milk you can express is a really poor way to judge how much milk you are producing. This is because babies milk your breast much better than a pump or hand.

'Test weighing' is another poor measure of how much milk your baby is getting. This involves weighing the baby before and after a feed, to estimate how much milk she is getting and what the milk supply is like. Test weighing to judge the milk supply is only accurate if carried out at every feed, over a period of at least 24 hours.

Test weighing at just one feed will not tell you whether your baby is getting enough milk overall. Nor will it tell you how much milk your baby needs. This varies from baby to baby. The wet and dirty nappy count will tell you whether or not your milk supply is adequate for your baby's needs.

Checklist to tell your baby is getting enough breastmilk:
✓ at least 5 heavily-wet disposable nappies or at least 6 pale, very wet cloth/reusable nappies in 24 hours
✓ regular soft bowel motions
✓ good skin tone and bright eyes
✓ generally content even if sometimes fussy and unsettled
✓ gaining weight and growing in length and head circumference.

CHAPTER 7

Getting started

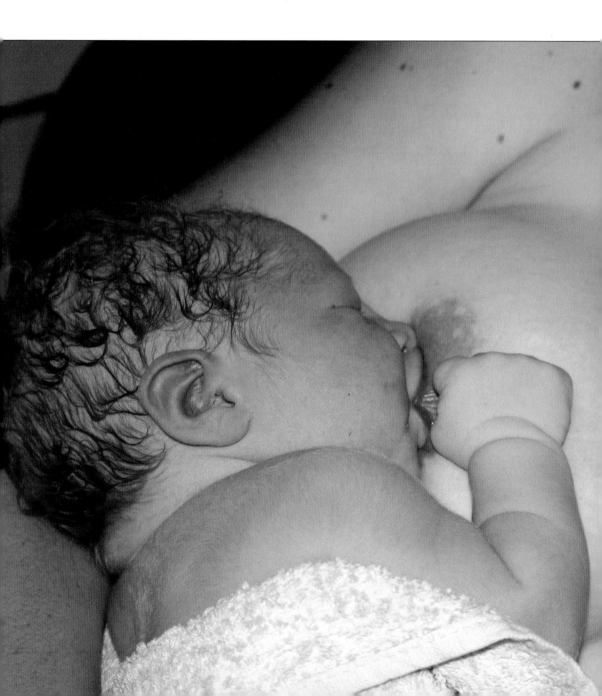

The first breastfeeds

A less than perfect start

Complementary feeds
and supplements

Night feeds

Engorgement

Leaking breasts

Sore nipples

Asking for advice

Getting to know your baby

The birth of your baby will probably be the most challenging and magical experience of your life, especially if this is your first baby. The first few days will be a blur — excitement at finally having your baby in your arms, tiredness as you begin to recover from labour and birth and lots of new things to learn.

To add to this, you will probably have to deal with a steady stream of visitors, an unfamiliar hospital or birth centre (where everyone but you seems to be an expert), a baby who needs you around the clock, and a body which is changing to nurture your newborn.

The first breastfeeds

Newborn babies are usually at their most alert and responsive in the first hour after birth. They have a strong urge to suck (you may have seen photos of babies in the womb sucking their fingers). Your baby's first feed should be as soon as he shows he is ready.

> **Mothers who breastfeed or have skin-to-skin contact with their babies within the first 2 hours of birth are more likely to go on to breastfeed successfully.**

When a baby is placed skin-to-skin with his mother immediately following his birth, he will in his own time:
- stop crying and lie alert and relaxed on his mother's tummy
- start moving around showing signs he wants to feed (sucking movements, hand-to-mouth movements)
- move up to the breast, make massage-like hand movements, and rub and lick the nipple and areola
- attach himself and start to breastfeed.

> **Your baby's actions help the nipple to become more erect so that it is easier for him to latch on. This raises the levels of oxytocin, helps the uterus contract and starts the milk flowing.**

There is also an increase of blood flow to the skin of your breasts. This makes your chest the ideal place to keep him warm.

Keeping mother and baby together
There are good reasons for keeping a baby covered, but unwrapped, on his mother's chest.

- Continuous skin-to-skin contact increases a baby's ability to suck correctly at the breast.
- Skin-to-skin contact helps maintain his temperature. A baby's body temperature will remain closer to normal when he is in contact with his mother than if he's in a cot. Even if his temperature is low, he will warm up more quickly on his mother's chest than in an incubator. He's also less likely to overheat. The temperature of a mother's chest changes to meet the needs of her baby.
- A baby kept with his mother maintains normal blood sugar levels. These can fall if he's separated from her.
- Skin-to-skin contact regulates his heart rate and breathing.
- Babies in contact with their mothers spend little time crying. Newborns who are separated from their mothers cry 10 times more frequently.
- Both mother and baby are calmer. Skin-to-skin contact helps you bond with your baby.
- Your newborn will spend time looking at your face and turn toward the sound of your voice. He wants your attention, to hear you talk to him, and to touch and smell you.
- Mothers who have their baby sleeping next to them behave differently to women whose babies are kept in a hospital nursery. They look at their babies more, talk to them more and touch then more. They talk less to others around them.
- 'Rooming-in' mothers are more aware of their babies' needs. They are better at recognising hunger cues.
- Babies who stay with their mothers are more likely to be still breastfeeding at 6 weeks.

A less than perfect start

For a variety of reasons, mothers and babies don't always get the perfect start to breastfeeding.
- Medical interventions during labour and birth make it difficult for you to move and handle your baby. It can be worse if you have had a caesarean delivery.
- You might feel shy about asking to have your baby with you, skin-to-skin. You may be afraid to 'bother' the hospital staff, particularly if they're busy helping other mothers.
- Drugs given during labour can interfere with your baby's instincts to breastfeed and your ability to care for him.
- A baby may be sleepy after a long labour or a stressful birth.

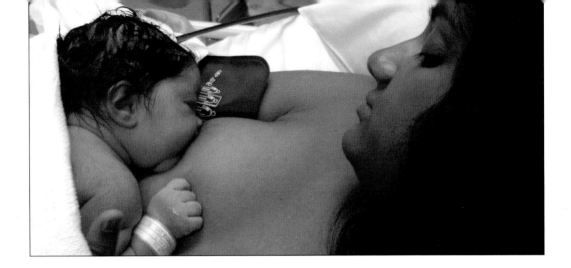

- Jaundice can also make a baby sleepy and slow to feed.
- Giving your baby formula or water, even in small amounts, can reduce the amount of breastmilk he takes.
- Sometimes you (and those around you) get anxious if your baby isn't feeding straight away. With the best of intentions, someone may try to get your baby to attach by pushing his head onto your breast. If he's not ready, he is not likely to attach well. Babies respond to pressure on the back of their heads by arching away from the breast, making attachment impossible. If you force a baby to the breast in this way, he may learn to associate the breast with an unpleasant experience.

Pain relief during labour

While some mothers choose to have no drugs during childbirth, others see pain relief as essential. The decision about pain relief needs to be an informed one, balancing the risks and benefits.

All women should receive information antenatally about the effects analgesia (pain relief) and anaesthetics may have on their baby. Talk with your doctor, midwife and partner about all the options for managing pain during labour. Discuss how the amount and timing of any drugs given during labour will affect you and your baby. Nitrous oxide ('gas'), opioids (mostly pethidine) and epidurals are the most commonly used pain relievers in Australia.

- **Nitrous oxide** leaves the body quickly, via the lungs. It is believed not to affect the baby.
- **Pethidine** is a synthetic version of morphine. There are a number of common side effects for the mother. These include sedation, dizziness, nausea and vomiting, respiratory depression and low blood pressure. Pethidine also affects the baby and is very likely to lead to a delay in establishing breastfeeding. Your

baby will be less likely to attempt to breastfeed in the hour after his birth. His breathing and sucking reflex may be affected.

- **Epidurals** contain a local anaesthetic combined with an opiate. Up to one third of Australian women have an epidural, especially if it is their first baby. An epidural will provide pain relief and can allow you to rest and relax during labour. There are, however, a number of breastfeeding-related issues to consider.
  - You won't be able to move much because you'll be hooked up to a machine to monitor the baby and a drip to administer the drugs.
  - The drugs pass through your bloodstream and the placenta to the baby. They will remain in his system for many days.
  - An epidural can affect the release of your own natural oxytocin, which triggers the let-down reflex and helps with bonding.
  - A baby's alertness and ability to settle can be affected.

Jaundice

A baby becomes jaundiced when his body is having trouble breaking down or getting rid of bilirubin. This is a compound produced when foetal red blood cells are replaced by normal red blood cells. It is yellow in colour, which is why babies with jaundice look yellow. It is normal for a newborn to have fairly high levels of bilirubin, as it comes from a natural process and has an antioxidant action. As long as the baby is able to feed frequently and get colostrum, it resolves itself. It is estimated that between 30–75% of babies develop some level of measurable jaundice. Babies whose mothers had pethidine during labour are more likely to have jaundice.

- **Physiological (or 'normal') jaundice** — is by far the most common form of jaundice in healthy newborn babies. It appears on day 3 or 4 and can be gone by day 7. It usually requires no special treatment, just frequent breastfeeds. Breastfeeding helps resolve jaundice because colostrum has a natural laxative effect. It helps your baby pass meconium and get rid of excess bilirubin from his body.

  Bad feeding advice, such as limiting the amount of colostrum and breastmilk your baby receives in the first few days, can affect this type of jaundice. Breastmilk, rather than water, is the best way of reducing bilirubin. Giving water can increase bilirubin levels. Water also reduces your baby's desire for the breast and therefore your milk supply. Babies affected by jaundice are usually very sleepy. They need to be encouraged to feed often.

- **Breastmilk jaundice** — very occasionally, a substance in breastmilk seems to cause jaundice. In these otherwise healthy babies, bilirubin levels rise on days 4–7, peak at 2 weeks and then slowly drop to normal between 4 and 16 weeks. No treatment is usually required, but phototherapy may be recommended if bilirubin levels rise above a certain limit. If you notice that your baby's skin or eyes are looking a bit yellow, you should contact your doctor who can check him for jaundice and measure his levels. In rare cases, you may also be advised to stop breastfeeding temporarily and feed him alternative milk until the bilirubin levels reduce. If this happens, expressing your milk will keep up your milk supply so that you can start breastfeeding again as soon as your baby's bilirubin levels allow.

- **Pathological jaundice** — this type of jaundice is not normal. It can be associated with some medical conditions. It can also occur after the use of a vacuum extractor or excessive bruising at birth. Some of these babies may need to be readmitted to hospital for treatment.

Encouraging a sleepy baby

A sleepy baby needs lots of encouragement to feed well. If he's sleeping next to you, you have the perfect opportunity to watch him for the first cues that he's ready to feed:

- rapid eye movements under the eyelids
- mouth and tongue movements
- hand-to-mouth movements
- body movements
- small sounds.

You can actively encourage him. Express a little colostrum by squeezing the areola firmly, about 30 mm back from the nipple. Let a few drops fall into your baby's mouth. Sometimes, this first taste is enough to get him interested. It may help a reluctant baby to persist and try to latch on. Sometimes, he will become more alert if you unwrap him or change his nappy. It also helps to have skin-to-skin contact or 'wear' him in a sling.

Complementary feeds and supplements

Your colostrum will nourish your baby well in the early days after birth. If he is allowed to feed frequently, he will not need any other fluids. Almost all babies lose weight in the first few days. This does not mean they need other fluids as well as breastmilk. Indeed they can lose more weight when given extra fluids in the early days.

If your baby is unsettled for any reason, some hospital staff may suggest a complementary feed (a top-up of infant formula or boiled water). It is very important to make it clear that you are fully breastfeeding and do not want this. Your baby does not need, and should not be given, extra fluids.

This means no water and particularly no infant formula, unless there is a compelling medical need for it. Any foreign fluid will reduce his appetite and his willingness to breastfeed. It will also mean that you will make less milk. If you or the baby's father have a family history of allergies, food intolerance or medical conditions such as asthma or diabetes, infant formula should only be given when prescribed by a paediatrician.

If your baby doesn't settle after a feed, you can try putting him back to the breast for a top-up.

Your body is making milk all the time and your breasts are never completely empty. A short top-up feed after 20 minutes or so may be all that's needed to settle your baby.

Night feeds

Before your baby was born, he was fed continuously through the placenta and never knew what it was to be hungry. Once he is born he loses the warmth and support of your womb. Suddenly, he has a strange gnawing feeling inside, a new and urgent feeling of hunger. Unlike an adult stomach, his stomach is very tiny (about the size of his own clenched fist), so it doesn't hold much. Breastmilk is also extremely well absorbed. It is easy to understand why a baby can't go long without being fed.

This is why you will need to feed him at night, as well as during the day. Most newborn babies need feeding several times during the night. This may continue for weeks or months, depending on your baby's individual needs. Night feeds are also important for your milk supply.

Having your baby sleep next to you, or nearby, makes it easier to respond when he stirs for a feed. You'll quickly get to know his cues.

Leaving him to cry can make him too upset to feed well. If you respond quickly to the early signs, it won't be too long before you are both asleep again. Feeding at night keeps you comfortable. You will sleep better because your breasts are not tight and engorged.

I found it really hard to sleep on those painful lumpy breasts, so I gazed hopefully down on my little one, hoping she would wake up, have a little feed and take some of this pain away — enough for me to get some sleep too.

Engorgement

Many mothers have engorged breasts when their milk comes in. It is not only the amount of milk that increases, but also other fluids in the breast, including the increased blood supply needed to get full milk production started.

> **Your breasts may feel huge, tight and quite uncomfortable. Engorgement makes it hard for your baby to attach well.**

There are a number of ways to relieve engorgement:
- **Feed your baby frequently.** Feeding often is the best way to prevent your breasts getting too full. It also relieves any fullness that does happen. You need to feed at least 3-hourly (including during the night). If you can add extra feeds when you first notice your breasts starting to become tight, that's even better. If your breasts become full and uncomfortable, you may need to wake your baby or pick him up to feed as soon as you see him stirring.
- **Let your baby set the length of each feed.** Don't limit his sucking time.
- **Avoid giving other fluids.** Your baby doesn't need top-ups of infant formula or water unless there is a compelling medical reason.
- **Take your bra off completely before beginning to breastfeed.** Babies feed better if they have unrestricted access to the breast, with lots of skin-to-skin contact. If your breasts are very full, feeding without a bra is much more comfortable. When you are wearing one, make sure it supports your breasts and is not too tight (you shouldn't see marks from seams or edges).

- **Use warm compresses before feeds,** expressing a little milk under a warm shower or stroking your breast from the chest wall towards the nipple, all help make feeding easier.
- **Express a little before feeds** if your baby has trouble latching and staying on. If your breasts are too full and tight, your nipple may not stand out well. Hand expressing a little may soften your breast so that your baby can attach more easily.
- **Reverse pressure softening** *(based on work by K Jean Cotterman RNC IBCLC)* can be used to soften overfull breasts before feeding or expressing (it works best when mother is lying on her back). Make sure you have short fingernails so you don't damage your breast tissue. Place several fingers flat on the sides of your breast and close to your nipple with first knuckles touching the nipple. Push in and hold for 1–3 minutes or more. Repeat above and below the nipple.

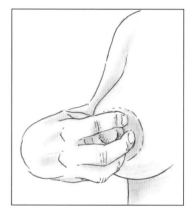

   You can also use all of your fingertips on one hand to push the breast tissue in around the whole nipple. Maintain this pressure for 1–3 minutes or more, until the tissue softens beneath them.

With your breast softened around the nipple and areola, your baby will be able to draw your nipple well into his mouth. This will prevent him from chewing on it. It is also likely to trigger your let-down reflex.

- **Massage the breast** gently while you are feeding. Without interrupting your baby or making it harder for him to stay attached, stroke your breast smoothly from the chest wall down towards the nipple. Be sure to handle your breasts gently as they bruise more easily when they're engorged.
- **Use cold packs after a feed** to keep you feeling comfortable. Place cold packs or a frozen (water-filled) disposable nappy over the affected breast(s). You can also use thoroughly washed and dried, crisp, cold cabbage leaves (remove the large veins first). Studies into the use of cabbage leaves haven't yet revealed why they help reduce the swelling. They may contain some special substance or they may just work because they are cold. However, many mothers find them soothing. Don't try them if you have an allergy or sensitivity to cabbage.
- **If necessary, express after feeds.** In cases of very painful engorgement, you may be advised to empty your breasts (as far as possible), by hand expressing

or using an electric breast pump. This sometimes eases the swelling within the breast. The lactation consultant at the hospital can help you with this.

- **Ask for pain relief** if you feel you need it.

Leaking breasts

Leaking breasts are very common in the first few weeks. They usually settle down as the muscles in your nipples develop and control the flow of milk better. Sometimes leaking can go on for longer, especially if you are producing a bit more milk than your baby needs or if you have a very strong let-down reflex.

There are several things you can do to deal with leaking breasts:
- **Use nursing pads.** All new mothers are told to have a box of nursing pads ready. Some women leak very little and only a few are used. Others will be sending their partners out to bulk buy. Many women need breast pads in their bra or singlet top full-time (even in bed) and may even have to change them between feeds.

  Avoid any nursing pads that hold moisture against the skin, as these can cause soggy nipples that are more likely to become sore or cracked. Make sure your bra is roomy enough to hold whatever sort of pad you choose without putting pressure on your breasts. If you wear your bra to bed, take care that it doesn't dig in when you are lying down as this may lead to blocked milk ducts.
- **Catch the overflow** while you're feeding. Use a clean cloth to catch any milk that leaks out of one breast while your baby feeds from the other. Avoid using tissues or other synthetic fibres as these can rub or stick to your skin.
- **Stop the flow when necessary.** If your milk starts to leak when you are away from your baby or unable to feed for some reason, you can stop the overflow. Press firmly on your nipple with your hand or forearm for several seconds when the let-down reflex starts. Crossing your arms can be a discreet way to do this. Try not to do this too often, as it may cause blockages in the milk ducts.

Sore nipples

Sore nipples in the first week (or in fact at any time) can certainly take the enjoyment out of breastfeeding. Fortunately this is usually short-lived. Some nipple pain with initial attachment is common in the early weeks of breastfeeding when the nipples are naturally more sensitive and getting used to the strong sucking of a healthy baby. It is now thought that the extra sensitivity is important for the release of hormones to get milk production going.

Sometimes mothers are still told that limiting feeds will lessen any early soreness. This is not correct. Restricting your baby's time at the breast leads to a build-up of milk and increased engorgement, resulting in even more problems. Most mothers find their nipples adjust to their new job and improve quickly.

If your nipples are very painful, or the pain lasts beyond the initial attachment, or your nipples are cracked, red, blistered or bruised, it is very likely that your baby is not attaching to the breast properly. This not only makes it painful for you, but may also stop your baby from getting the milk he needs. If the information in Chapter 5 is not enough to solve the problem, it is time to seek skilled help from an ABA counsellor, a lactation consultant, child health nurse or your medical adviser.

There are a few extra things that can reduce the risk of early nipple soreness:
- **Express a little colostrum or milk onto the nipple** at the end of a feed. Leave your bra open until it dries naturally. Go without a bra sometimes.
- Your skin is more easily damaged when it is either too dry or too moist, so **keeping nipples healthy and supple** is important in preventing soreness.
- If your breasts leak milk between feeds, **change your bra, pads and clothing** so they don't become soggy.
- Special glands in the areola produce natural oils that clean and lubricate the nipples. **Rinsing with water** in your daily bath or shower is all that is needed.
- **Your breastmilk is the best 'nipple cream'.** Commercially produced creams and ointments can contain ingredients that a baby should not swallow. They can also harbour germs such as *Candida* (thrush). They are not needed unless they are prescribed for a medical reason.

Asking for advice

Most women feel vulnerable after the birth of a baby. Just when you need help most, it seems harder to ask for it. In the first few days and weeks after giving birth, your hormone levels change rapidly and so do your moods. One day you will be on a high, the next in the depths of despair. Even though you are confident and competent in other areas, you may be shocked to find that you feel unsure in dealing with your own baby. Even if you are familiar with babies, each one is different. You and your baby need to learn about each other.

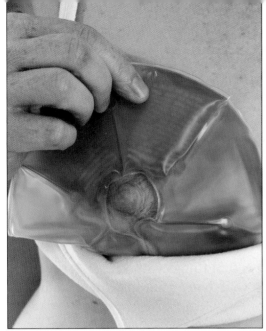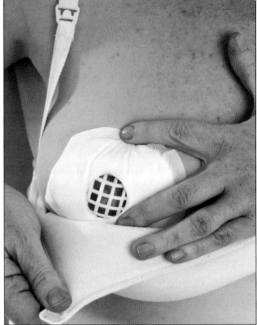

Gel ice breast pad for applying cold to the breast (left) and absorbent breast pad with woven filter to 'air' the nipple (right).

It was difficult with a newborn baby and painful breasts to arrange to go and see a stranger about breastfeeding problems. I was lucky to find people I felt comfortable with, but also received lots of different advice. This was useful, as it gave me more options to try, but also frustrating while I was still learning and struggling.

Even though you ask for advice, you don't have to follow it all. You will probably hear a range of opinions. Try the ones that you think will suit you and ignore those that don't seem to work. The best outcome is for you to feel able to make decisions and take control of your new life.

Why advice can be conflicting

Sometimes it can seem that every time you ask for advice you hear something different. There are a number of reasons for this:

- The first days and weeks of your baby's life are times of rapid change. Advice will change almost as rapidly as your baby is growing. A baby's needs at 1 day or 1 week are vastly different from those of a 6-week-old baby. These are different again from those of a 3-month-old or a 6-month-old.
- Health professionals differ a great deal in their level of breastfeeding knowledge. Some have recent training in helping breastfeeding mothers while others base

their advice on what they learned when completing their qualification. These days there is a lot of research on breastfeeding and we're learning new things all the time. The advice that was accurate 5 years ago may now be very out-of-date.

You are the one who will come to know and understand your baby best. Listen to the 'experts', but listen to your own instincts too. Keep persevering till you get the help you need. *You are the 'expert' on your baby.*

Getting to know your baby

The only thing that you can be sure of is that things will change. It seems that as soon as you start to recognise your baby's patterns he develops new and different ones.

Your baby is not doing this deliberately to frustrate you. Babies are people too. Like grown-ups, their behaviour changes according to their needs. Babies grow so quickly. In their first year, they will grow at a greater rate than at any other time in their lives.

That tiny bundle that seemed content to just sleep and feed while you were in hospital may seem like a different person when you return home. He may cry more often, even after he's been fed and changed. You may feel unsure how to comfort him. This can be stressful at first, particularly because you are tired and feeling fragile yourself.

Babies take time to adapt to their environment and even small changes can cause them to react. At home, you may have other responsibilities. Your baby may be missing that 'cocooned' time in hospital, when he was your only responsibility and you were able to attend to him without delay.

You will sometimes feel that looking after your baby and fulfilling your own needs is an impossible balancing act. It is reassuring to know that offering the breast will satisfy both his appetite and his need for closeness. It may be difficult to believe at first, but as you get to know each other and his system matures, your baby and your life will become more predictable.

I loved the serenity of being able to sit, undisturbed, just gazing at my beautiful baby and marvel at his very being.

CHAPTER 8

Special deliveries

Caesarean delivery

Premature babies

Twins

Babies who are sick or have
a disability

Even though we know that things don't always go to plan, we expect to have a gentle calm birth, a picture-perfect baby and a smooth transition to parenthood. Giving birth prematurely, perhaps by caesarean delivery, can be quite a shock. If you have found out that you are expecting two babies (or even more!) you may well be wondering how on earth you will cope. What if the thing we all dread the most happens and we find ourselves with a baby who is very sick or has a disability? Then the picture we have of ourselves as a mother may just vanish.

Breastfeeding can be a lifeline to you as you come to terms with what being a mother will be like for you.

Caesarean delivery

Thirty percent of Australia babies are born by caesarean section, which is three times the rate recommended by the World Health Organization. So it's worth taking a moment to think about breastfeeding after a caesarean delivery. Don't let anyone tell you that you can't breastfeed. While there may be short-term effects from your baby's caesarean delivery, you can breastfeed as well as a mother who has had a vaginal birth. Even if you get off to a slower start, you will most likely catch up before the end of your baby's first week.

After elective (planned) caesarean births, babies are usually quite alert. Emergency caesareans may be more stressful for both mother and baby. The type of anaesthetics used will depend on the circumstances. An epidural anaesthetic or spinal block is most common, which means you are awake and alert throughout. Mothers who have an epidural can usually breastfeed soon after delivery.

Drugs used for anaesthesia will have some effect on you and your baby. You can read about this in Chapter 7. People often think that a mother's milk is slower to 'come in' after a caesarean. However, milk production switches on after a baby is born because of the removal of the placenta. This changes the balance of hormones in the blood.

In many hospitals the baby is placed in skin-to-skin contact with the mother while she is still on the operating table. As soon as the paediatrician has checked the baby, she is placed under the sterile drapes on her mother's chest. This skin-to-skin contact allows your baby get to know your feel and scent and helps the early establishment of breastfeeding. If this is not possible, your partner can hold your baby till you are able to.

Not every caesarean mother can start breastfeeding straight away. The baby may be premature or unwell and need time in special care. In some cases, it may be several hours or even days before you can put her to the breast. You can ask for help with expressing your colostrum and, later, your breastmilk, if it comes in before she is able to breastfeed. After a caesarean it can be tempting not to feed your baby overnight. However, it is important for your baby to receive your colostrum and to begin breastfeeding.

> **Frequent feeds in the first days after birth, including during the night, mean that she starts learning to breastfeed while your breasts are still soft and easier for her to attach to. Night feeds also help to prevent breast engorgement and to get your milk supply going.**

Let the hospital staff know that you wish to spend as much time with your baby as possible. For the first day or so, you may have a drip for pain relief and fluids and a catheter to drain your bladder. While these are in place, you may need a little help with holding your baby and breastfeeding. This is where your partner can help. Breastfeeding while sitting and holding your baby across your body can be uncomfortable at first. Try different positions until you find one that suits you both. See the section on twins that follows to get some ideas on other feeding positions.

If you're in pain, ask about pain relief that won't make your baby sleepy or less likely to suck strongly. This will in turn help your milk to flow — pain won't. The hospital physiotherapist can help you recover faster by teaching you exercises specially designed for caesarean mothers.

Once you leave the hospital, you will need time to return to your normal energy levels. Rest is very important — after all, you're recovering from an operation and adjusting to life as a new mother at the same time.

Premature babies

Unless there have been warning signs during pregnancy, most parents expect their babies to arrive around the due date. So a premature birth can come as a shock. Many parents of a premature baby are not at all ready for the early arrival. Instead of cuddling and breastfeeding your baby, you may have to wait hours just to see her. You may be extremely worried about whether she will even survive. She may be sent to a different hospital in another city.

Your breastmilk is the one thing only you can provide for your baby. Being able to be in charge of this vital part of her care can be a positive outlet for your feelings.

If your baby is not yet ready to breastfeed, she can still be given your breastmilk. The suck/swallow reflex does not fully develop until somewhere between 32 and 40 weeks gestation, so it may take a while for a premature baby to breastfeed. Some babies are fed intravenously for a while. Most receive their mother's expressed milk through a feeding tube into the stomach that passes through either the nose or mouth. They can begin breastfeeding when they are able to suck and swallow properly. Starting with tiny amounts, a baby will gradually receive more breastmilk. Parents can assist with tube-feeds. It will give you confidence in handling your baby. If your baby is being tube-fed, ask if you can cuddle her skin-to-skin near your nipple as she is being fed. She will soon start searching for your nipple and may latch on and suck. Sucking is important for all newborn babies. Sucking while being tube-fed also aids digestion.

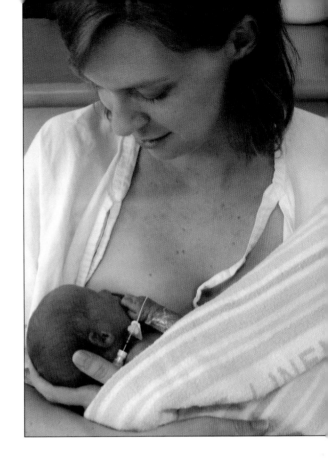

Until you can feed your baby directly from your breast, you will need to express your breastmilk. Every drop you can express will help her. Start expressing as soon as you can after the birth to build your milk supply.

If you can build a full milk supply in the early days, you are less likely to have problems with milk supply later. This will help make sure you have enough milk for your baby as her needs increase.

Freshly-expressed breastmilk is best for your baby, as freezing and thawing change some of the factors in the milk. Thawed breastmilk is the next best food and ensures that you will always have breastmilk ready when she needs it, even if you cannot be with her. Sometimes very tiny babies may need extra vitamins, iron and other nutrients added to their breastmilk. This does not mean that there is anything wrong with your milk. Your baby just needs a little boost because she is so very tiny. This is to make up for what she would have received in your womb if she had not been born so early.

There are many reasons why breastmilk is vital for premature babies:
- Although similar in many respects to full-term breastmilk, 'pre-term' milk contains higher amounts of protein and other nutrients vital for premmie growth and health.
- The nutrients in the milk of mothers of premature babies are suited to their babies' stage of development.
- Breastmilk helps protect babies from infections.
- Breastmilk helps protect premature babies from necrotising enterocolitis and sepsis.
- Breastfeeding is less stressful for the premature baby than bottle-feeding. Even a very small premature baby can be at the breast for long periods without distress.
- While a baby is at the breast, she stays warm. The oxygen levels in her blood remain normal during and after feeds.
- Breastmilk is easy to digest, so is less taxing on her immature digestive system than any other food.
- Getting rid of the small amount of waste will not overtax her immature kidneys.
- A premature baby at the breast has long periods of closeness with the mother, including touching and eye-to-eye contact. During this time there are periods of sucking and resting. The touching and eye-to-eye contact they share during breastfeeds are vital to their long-term relationship. She should have as much time as she needs for a breastfeed or even just to cuddle, unless there are medical reasons to limit that time.

Skin-to-skin (kangaroo) care
Many hospitals around the world use a method of care for premature babies called 'kangaroo care'. Kangaroo care is offered to a stable premature baby, usually for a few hours a day and sometimes for much longer periods of time. Some hospitals offer this skin-to-skin contact even to some babies still attached to the ventilator. The baby, wearing only a nappy and a hat, is placed against the mother's skin underneath her clothing. Here she has free access to her mother's breasts. Fathers can also have this skin-to-skin contact with their baby.

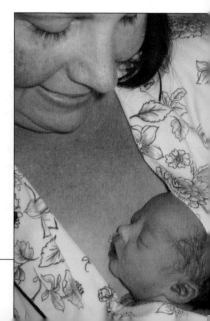

Skin-to-skin care has enormous benefits for babies:

- A baby maintains her body temperature and conserves energy (because these babies cry less and sleep more).
- She often begins breastfeeding much sooner than a baby cared for in an incubator.
- It increases the mother's breastmilk supply by an average of 50%.
- The baby's suckling ability improves.
- It helps the bonding between the baby and her parents, who become more confident caring for their baby.
- The baby tends to be more content at home, too.

If your baby's hospital doesn't use this method of care, speak with the staff about it. You may be able to at least hold your baby more often once she is stable enough.

'Real' breastfeeds

Your baby's first 'real' breastfeeds are an important step. Once she starts to develop a mature sucking and swallowing reflex, is strong enough and can control her body temperature (while you hold her close), she will be ready for this new adventure. You may start to notice cues that she is ready to feed. These include licking her lips, trying to put her hand to her mouth, and waking and crying regularly for feeds.

> **Babies can go from tube-feeding to the breast without ever having bottles. Breastfeeding is less stressful than bottle-feeding.**

The sucking pattern of a premature baby differs from that of a full-term baby. She will most likely start feeding with short bursts of sucking and long pauses in between. These might be rhythmic, slow sucking or fast, flutter sucking or a mixture of both. Don't expect too much at first — even if all that happens is your baby licks your nipples and has a few small sucks, you are on your way. As she matures, she will suck for longer and her sucking will get stronger.

Many premature babies have attachment problems. This is often due to a receding chin, thin cheeks and a small mouth. Less fat in a premature baby's cheeks makes it harder for her to get a good grip on the breast. Sometimes, a thin nipple shield can help the baby to stay attached. Ask a hospital lactation consultant to help you with positioning and attachment.

Going home without your baby

Going home without your baby is upsetting. Focus on the positive aspects of going home, such as having more time to sleep, to express and to talk with your partner about your feelings.

All the time my baby was in hospital I didn't feel part of reality. I was expected to carry on life as if it was normal but all the time I was away from the hospital, there was a part of me in the special care nursery with my baby.

When your baby finally comes home it can feel a bit like an anticlimax. You may not have the usual round of visitors or congratulations. People may not like to ask about the baby in case they upset you. Let them know that this is still a special occasion for you. Some parents feel that no-one really understands what they went through in hospital. It may help to join a support group for the parents of premature babies.

Twins

Sometimes it takes months to get used to the idea of having one baby. Twins may be twice as exciting — and twice as daunting. If twins are common in your family (and it's often the case), you may be able to talk to other parents in your family about how they managed. You may wonder whether you really will be able to breastfeed both babies. Can one woman produce enough milk? **Yes, she can!**

Remember that breastfeeding works on a supply and demand basis — **the more milk that is taken, the more that is made.** So if you feed your babies often, you won't have any trouble making plenty of milk for them.

> Breastfeeding is doubly important if your twins are premature, weak or small. If they are in the special care nursery, you will need to express your milk to get your supply going.

Express at least as often as you would feed a new baby — 8–10 or more times a day, including at least once at night. If only one of your babies is in care, express from the 'spare' breast while the other baby is feeding. Switch breasts at each feed. Your breastfeeding baby will trigger the let-down reflex, making it easier to express from the other breast.

Hold everything! I'm feeding

Breastfeeding twins requires a little extra planning. Regardless of the feeding position you choose, you may need extra pillows or large cushions. Some mothers find pillows designed for feeding twins useful. The Australian Multiple Birth Association may be able to give you more information about these and other helpful resources.

There are several different ways you can position your twins for feeding, including the classic twin hold (also called the football or under-arm hold), the parallel hold and the front 'V' hold. Each position is quite simple, as shown in the photos on the right. The one that suits you best will depend on the ages and stages of your babies.

Twin, football or under-arm hold

This position is the easiest to use when you don't have anyone around to help you. It is probably the most practical position for small babies, leaving two hands free. It puts no pressure on your tummy if you have had a caesarean. Lay your babies with their feet facing backwards or to the sides and tucked under your arms. Their faces will be towards yours. If you are sitting up, support your babies with your palms behind their shoulders and

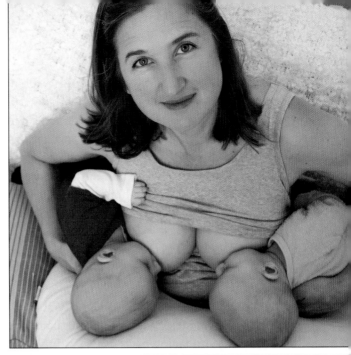

Twin, football or underarm hold (top), V-hold (bottom left) and parallel hold (bottom right)

with your fingers to guide their heads. Lift them to your breasts (one baby at a time while they need help attaching). Use your elbows to hug your babies to you. Raise your knees high enough to ensure that a pillow on your lap will support the babies' heads at your breasts without you having to lean over. This will leave your hands free. If you are reclining, position each baby, one at a time close to the breast and with her feet at your side and allow each baby to self-attach. Provide support where needed with your hands and arms.

Parallel hold

This is more discreet than the twin hold, but harder to manage when your babies are young. When they are older, you can feed like this without pillows, as one baby's body will support the head of the other. This makes it more convenient when you are feeding away from home. Hold the first baby in the normal cradle position (across your lap). Lay the second baby gently on the body of, and parallel to, the first baby, so that her head is at your other breast and supported with your hand behind her shoulders if needed. Both babies will be lying in the same direction. If you need to support your arms as you hold your babies, raise your knees.

Front 'V' hold

This is a good method for feeding at night and helpful if you cannot sit comfortably after the birth. If you are sitting up, it may be hard with tiny babies, as you will have limited control over their heads. However, if you are lying back, this should make it easier for your babies. Make sure your back is well supported. Place a baby at each breast so they are facing each other and their knees are bent and touching. Support their backs with your arms while your hands cup their bottoms.

One or two babies at a time?

You may be wondering whether to feed your babies together or one at a time, to keep each to his or her own breast, or to switch sides.

> There is no one right way and how you do it is as much up to your babies as you. Most mothers do a bit of both, depending on the babies' ages.

If you feed one baby at a time:

- It allows you to focus on positioning and attaching each baby and may be easier and more comfortable for you at first.
- You will be more mobile, so you can tend to other children if need be.
- The down-sides include:
  - You may spend twice as much time feeding. It may feel as if you always have a baby at the breast.
  - If both babies need a feed at the same time, it may be difficult to relax and feed one while the other is upset.
  - It can be hard to settle one baby if the other is crying for a feed.

If you feed both babies at the same time:

- It calms both babies and you can relax once you get the hang of it.

- Usually one baby feeds from only one breast each time. This means that feeding may take even less time than for the single baby, who feeds from both sides with a rest between sides. However, some babies may need more sucking time.
- The down-sides include:
  - Finding a comfortable feeding position might be hard and you might need another person to help in the first weeks.
  - Your babies may be quite different and have different feeding needs, so they may not always want to feed at the same time. You may have to wake the second baby to feed and not all babies feed well when woken. However, many babies soon adapt and feed together well.
  - In summer, you may feel hot with pillows and babies all round you. A fan blowing near your face will help move the air and make you feel more comfortable.
  - It can be harder to find suitable spots where you can feed when you are away from home.

If you are giving each baby their own breast, keep in mind:
- If one baby does not suck as well as the other, you may find it better to switch breasts to help the weaker baby.
- Babies need equal right and left visual stimulation. If each baby always feeds from the same breast, you should vary positions at that breast. One way is to use the underarm hold sometimes and the normal cradle hold at other times. If you can carry or burp the babies in different positions, this will also help.
- Some women find that their breasts make different amounts of milk, so one baby may always get less. This can be an advantage for babies with different needs. If they are fed according to need, this won't affect the total intake over a day.

Triplets, quads or more!
Thanks to IVF, multiple births are now more common. If the idea of breastfeeding one baby seems like a challenge and feeding two sounds demanding, then feeding three or more will sound alarming. However, it can be done. Some women are able to produce enough milk to meet all their babies' needs and almost all are able to meet most of them. If breastfeeding is what you've always wanted, then being able to breastfeed these babies will be even more rewarding, as mothers of multiples have discovered. All of the information and ideas in the previous sections of this chapter will apply if you are expecting more than two babies. More help can be found on this topic in ABA's booklet *Breastfeeding: twins, triplets and more*.

Babies who are sick or have a disability

Babies with Down syndrome

Down syndrome is the most common genetic disorder in human babies. Its effect on children varies widely. Generally they achieve the normal milestones but a little more slowly.

> **If you have just found out that your baby has Down syndrome, you will have mixed emotions. This is a natural reaction as you wonder what lies ahead for you all.**

Breastfeeding will offer your baby much more than nutrition:

- It provides food, comfort and stimulates all of the baby's senses.
- Breastfeeding strengthens the muscles of the baby's lips, tongue and face. This prepares the baby for eating other foods and later for speech.
- Breastmilk does not hurt the airways if it gets into them. Breastfed babies have fewer ear infections.

If your baby has problems with breastfeeding at first, persistence and time will help her (and you) to learn.

Other points to be aware of:

- Babies with Down syndrome tend to have low muscle tone and so may have trouble getting their mouth around the nipple and attaching correctly to the breast.
- Some babies may also have trouble coordinating their sucking, swallowing and breathing. This may cause them to gulp and choke as they feed.
- They may get less milk for their efforts and they often get tired quickly. This can and will improve with time and patience. The action of breastfeeding itself will improve your baby's muscle strength, which will help make up for the low tone.
- As your baby gets stronger and learns to breastfeed better, she will be able to drink more milk. It is important that you make sure your baby is getting enough milk. If you are worried about any of this, see your medical adviser straight away. Note that there are special growth charts for babies with Down syndrome: *growthcharts.com/charts/DS/charts.htm*
- If you can start your milk flowing before you offer your baby your breast, she will not have to spend energy sucking for little result. Make sure she is well positioned at your breast and that her body is well supported. This will help her use most of her energy for feeding.

- Supporting your breast and her chin while she feeds may help your baby stay attached. Cup your hand under your breast and then slide it forward so that three fingers support your breast. Make a U-shape with your thumb and first finger and support her jaw in that U. This position is called the Dancer Hand.

ABA has a helpful booklet, *Breastfeeding: your baby with Down syndrome.*

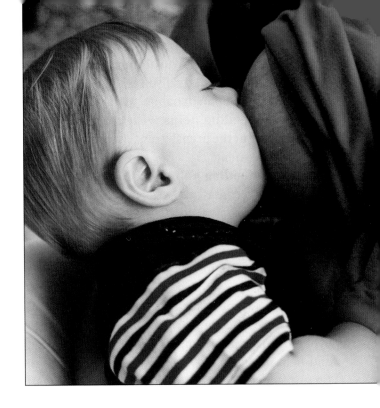

Babies with a cleft lip and/or palate

Finding that your baby has a cleft is a great shock. When you start thinking how you will manage, some of your first questions may be about feeding and whether a baby with a cleft lip and/or palate can be breastfed.

> **Most babies with a cleft lip only can breastfeed with the soft breast tissue filling the gap. The most important thing to know is that even if your baby cannot breastfeed at first, you can still feed her your own breastmilk.**

When you are in hospital with your baby, there will be staff and breast pumps to help you express milk for her. If you are feeling stressed or upset, it may seem easier not to breastfeed or express milk. However, breastmilk and breastfeeding are very important for your baby, both now and in the future.

- **Formula-fed babies have more infections.** Babies with a cleft palate can have ear infections more often than other babies, as the Eustachian tubes (that go from the back of the nose to the ear) can fill with milk when they swallow. Breastmilk protects babies from infection. This is very important for babies who may need surgery.

- **Breastmilk is a natural fluid.** It will not hurt the delicate lining of your baby's nose. Breastmilk is also less harmful than formula if breathed into the lungs. This is common in babies with feeding problems.
- **Breastfeeding helps with correct face and jaw development.** Your baby's sucking at the breast uses the right facial muscles. It also helps her future speech development.
- **Breastfeeding helps bonding.** Breastfeeding gives your baby lots of cuddling and skin contact.
- There are also post-surgery benefits. **Breastmilk contains lysozyme and epithelial growth factor that help to stop wounds getting infected.** Many babies are allowed to breastfeed straight after surgery. Breastfeeding provides comfort for your baby and your soft nipple will not hurt or damage her mouth.

All babies want to suckle a lot after birth. Your baby does not know she has a cleft and your breast is the perfect soft shape for her to suckle. Even if she is getting most of her milk from a cup or feeding bottle, sucking at the breast will exercise her muscles and help her get ready for breastfeeding once the cleft is repaired. ABA's booklet, *Breastfeeding: babies with a cleft of lip and/or palate*, contains a wealth of information and ideas on feeding techniques.

CHAPTER 9

Out and about with your breastfed baby

Breastfeeding away from home

Some practical suggestions

Coping with criticism

Travelling with your breastfed baby

Every single day, thousands of mothers are out and about with their breastfed babies. Breastfeeding is simply a normal and natural part of their everyday life. The 'portability' of breastfed babies is one of the great things about breastfeeding. You can take your baby with you anywhere and breastfeed anytime. You don't have to worry about having clean bottles, formula powder, access to clean water or bottle-warming facilities.

Mothers and babies have the right to breastfeed. There is legislation, both at federal and state level, to support this. For example, under the federal Sex Discrimination Act 1984, it is illegal to directly or indirectly discriminate against a woman on the ground of breastfeeding. The definition of breastfeeding includes expressing milk.

The needs of a baby are different to those of an adult. All mothers have the right to meet their baby's needs.

Breastfeeding away from home

Most people would think it silly to suggest that babies should wait for a feed until they were home from an outing or their mother found a baby care room. Yet many women (especially younger mothers) are anxious about breastfeeding in public places or near other people. This means they stay home with their breastfed babies or only go to large shopping centres. In almost every other area of their lives, women are confident and keen to stand up for their rights, but in this aspect of parenting many have been made to feel powerless and defensive. It's a major barrier to breastfeeding.

It is important for you to feel comfortable and relaxed wherever you breastfeed. In the early days, while you and your baby are still learning to breastfeed, feed times can sometimes be tricky. You might feel better feeding where it is a little more private, such as a baby care room. Some are little more than a chair in a cubicle off the public toilets, but if you are lucky there may be an ABA approved facility near you. These provide privacy and comfortable seating, hot and cold water and hand-drying facilities, somewhere clean and safe to change nappies and hygienic waste disposal — all in a smoke-free environment. For your nearest ABA Baby Care Room, check the website: *breastfeeding.asn.au>services>baby care rooms.* Alternatively, look for ABA's Breastfeeding Welcome Here sticker. The staff and management of these places welcome breastfeeding mothers. They are smoke-free and there is space for a pram.

While some mothers are glad of the privacy baby care rooms may offer, others prefer to breastfeed wherever they happen to be. Even the most basic baby care rooms are few and far between. Hungry babies don't want to wait for a feed while you search for somewhere to breastfeed out of sight. You'll end up very distressed and with a screaming baby. Everyone notices a screaming baby, while few people notice a baby quietly breastfeeding. You should be able to find a quiet seat in a café, the shopping centre, the park or a playground.

If you're out with your partner or meeting friends for a meal or coffee, you will want to do just that, not go somewhere else, by yourself, to feed your baby. Most new mothers feel nervous the first few times they feed their babies in public. It becomes easier with practice, even for mothers who said before their baby was born that they would never feed in front of other people.

Some practical suggestions

- If you want to get an idea of what others see when you are breastfeeding, practise at home, in front of a full-length mirror. You will probably be surprised by how little of your breasts show.
- Some types of clothing make it easier to breastfeed. Separates are ideal with tops that lift up rather than having to completely unbutton. Breastfeeding singlets are great, especially in cold weather, as your tummy stays covered.
- A bra that you can open using one hand helps you put your baby to the breast more easily.
- A lightweight bunny rug or a shawl can help cover your baby at your breast, particularly if he is easily distracted by what's happening nearby. This also works well if you have larger breasts.
- Feeding your baby just before you leave home might mean that all he needs is a quick 'top-up' later.
- A corner table where you can sit with your back to other diners can give you a bit more privacy.

Rather than being criticised, it's more likely that no-one will notice. You may even get compliments. The sight of a baby peacefully breastfeeding can bring out the best in people. You might be surprised by a smile from a stranger or an encouraging word.

Why the fuss?

While you may see stories in the media about someone objecting to breastfeeding in a public place, in fact, this rarely happens. Why is seeing a mother breastfeed her baby in public so confronting for some people? There may be a number of reasons:

- Newspapers, radio and television thrive on conflict and bad news. It is the essence of news reporting. The fact that things are going along smoothly is simply not news. That's why you rarely hear about the many mothers who happily breastfeed at work, in shopping centres, in parks, in restaurants, in trains or just about anywhere, without raising an eyebrow, let alone a ruckus.

- It is possible that many people have never seen a baby breastfeeding before. In Australia, it is mostly done in private, at home. This means young people do not often see breastfeeding. In fact, before becoming a mother many women have never seen a baby at the breast.

- You may be surprised to hear negative comments from other women. Perhaps the sight of another woman breastfeeding touches deep-seated emotions and beliefs about their own experience feeding their babies and what they have been taught is correct behaviour. Comments from men often involve asking the mother to move to a private breastfeeding area in the (usually misguided) belief that she will feel more comfortable.

- Some new fathers feel concerned about the idea of their partner breastfeeding around their mates (and sometimes even their family). They may think that you will be exposing your breasts and that men might 'perv' on you. They will be reassured when they see how little breast is actually showing.

- Some onlookers may be disturbed by the intimacy of the breastfeeding relationship. Many people associate physical intimacy with sex. The closeness between a mother and her breastfeeding baby may confuse and threaten them. They may feel that this should be kept private, that it belongs in the home, even perhaps in the bedroom, not out in the world.

- For many people, it's not the glimpse of a breast that they find confronting but the fact that milk is coming out of it. These are likely to be the ones who direct you to the toilets, confusing breastmilk with excretion. Breastfeeding is a natural bodily function, but breastmilk is not a waste product. It is a baby's food.

Coping with criticism

If you do receive criticism for breastfeeding in public, be outraged rather than let yourself be bullied. It gets much better results. Take it as an opportunity to educate them about you and your baby's rights. Every time someone sees you breastfeeding your baby, you take one small step towards making breastfeeding a part of normal everyday life for everyone. A former federal Sex Discrimination Commissioner said:

Common sense dictates that hungry babies be fed and parents have the right to choose the option of breastfeeding their children. It will be a particularly sad day when a woman is penalised for properly caring for her child in a public place.

Travelling with your breastfed baby

Breastfeeding makes life much easier for you while you are travelling. Your baby's meals are available, whenever they are needed, at just the right temperature.

If you are travelling overseas and need to be vaccinated or take preventative medications, make sure you tell your doctor that you are breastfeeding. Discuss any effects these medications may have on your baby. You will also need to discuss any special protection that your baby may need, although your breastmilk will play an important part in boosting his immune system.

When you travel by plane, feed your baby during take-off and landing, when the air pressure changes inside the plane. If he is unsettled your breasts will provide familiar comfort, as well as both food and drink. If you are going somewhere hot, make sure to drink plenty of fluids. Your baby may need more breastfeeds than usual.

If you are travelling by car, never feed your baby while the car is moving. This would involve one or both of you being unrestrained. This is illegal and dangerous. It is much safer and more pleasant to stop at a roadside spot. Car air conditioners can sometimes be very drying, so your baby may need extra feeds. If your car has no air conditioning, your baby can get quite hot in the back seat. Try to ensure he is always shaded from the back and side windows and offer him frequent feeds.

CHAPTER 10

Looking after yourself

Real life with a baby

Motherhood and mental health

Exercise and diet

Smoking

Alcohol

Recreational drugs

Prescription medications

Drug information services
in Australia

Over-the-counter remedies
and herbal preparations

Everyone tells you that things change after you have a baby. However, if you are like most people, you probably don't really believe this.

Babies are very time-consuming. Mothering is a 24-hour-a-day, 7-day-a-week job. You will have less time for yourself. Therefore, it is important to think about how you will manage your own health and wellbeing, while caring for your baby.

Real life with a baby

Pregnancy and motherhood are often painted as being blissful experiences. The reality of mothering is usually hidden from us. We may get a better idea of what life is like with a baby if we are close to other women who are mothers. But even then, we often only hear half the story. It's very common for women to tell half-truths about their experiences because they want to be seen as 'good' mothers.

From early childhood we build up images of what life with a baby will be like and what a 'good' mother is. We hear that 'mothers take care of everything' and 'a good mother is always there for her baby'. The media reinforces these myths. Magazines and TV are full of images of well-dressed and well-groomed women and their equally stylish, happy children. Celebrities appear to cope easily with the transition to motherhood. It's easy to believe that if you're not a 'yummy mummy', you're not trying hard enough.

If you find you can't live up to all this, you are likely to feel disappointed. You probably also have an idea of the type of parent your partner will be. Sometimes real life doesn't live up to the image.

Now is the time to be kind to yourself. Focus your energy on yourself and your family.

Motherhood and mental health

It's normal for your emotions to go up and down both before and after your baby is born. It's not normal to keep on feeling anxious or depressed. Some mothers battle these emotions in silence. They try hard to 'snap out of it', without knowing that they have little control over the way they are feeling. It is very important that all new parents recognise the symptoms of depression and ask for help as early as possible.

Postnatal depression

Although most of us have heard about postnatal depression, we find it hard to accept that it might actually happen to us. It is normal for all mothers to feel anxious, tired or down at different times when they have a new baby. Many mothers get the 'baby blues', especially in the early days — but postnatal depression lasts longer and is worse.

Postnatal depression is different for each mother. There may be feelings of depression, anxiety and sadness that don't go away. These feelings may appear suddenly or gradually, within the first 12 months of her baby's life. Symptoms can range from a mild feeling of sadness to a numbing depression. They affect her ability to function each day.

How breastfeeding can help:

- When you're really struggling, breastfeeding your baby may be the one thing you feel you can do well.
- When you're feeling stressed, sitting or lying down to breastfeed your baby can be soothing, relaxing and calming.
- When you're feeling distant from your baby and unsure how to relate to her, the physical and emotional closeness of breastfeeding can strengthen the bond between you.
- When you're feeling as though the baby likes everyone but you, that she doesn't need you and would be better off without you, breastfeeding helps remind you that only you can make her feel full and content.

At this point, I must say that in losing myself, only one thing kept me turning back. Love for my son was overwhelming. Throughout my ordeal I always felt close to him; bonded by caring for him and the shared breastfeeding experience. I didn't know who I was, and yet because I was breastfeeding, I must have been his mother. Therefore, in my rational thoughts, I realised that I was someone. I was a mother.

Depression support services

For a list of postnatal support services across Australia, go to the beyondblue (national depression initiative) website: *beyondblue.org.au* or call the Information line: 1300 22 4636 or contact PANDA (Post and Antenatal Depression Association) *www.panda.org.au*.

Exercise and diet

Exercise is important to your health and helps you feel good. Regular, moderate exercise gives you more energy, a greater sense of wellbeing and helps you juggle the demands of being a mother. It protects you against osteoporosis, diabetes and heart disease later in life.

If you are eating well, have lost weight, but still can't fit into your pre-pregnancy clothes, you may need to tighten and tone a few muscles that were stretched during pregnancy. You may need someone to care for your baby so you can do the type of exercise you enjoyed before becoming pregnant — your partner, parents or a friend. Perhaps you could swap care of your baby with another mother or hire a sitter. If you can't, try walking to the shops or the park with your baby in a pram or sling. Many recreation centres hold special classes for mothers with a crèche on site. Some parks now have exercise equipment.

Check with your doctor or physiotherapist before starting any exercise program. This is most important during pregnancy and the first 2 months after giving birth. Postnatal exercises designed for new mothers will help you regain your pre-pregnancy shape and avoid later problems, such as incontinence (weak bladder) and prolapse of the uterus.

Studies on the effects of exercise on milk supply have shown that moderate exercise is fine for breastfeeding mothers.

- Feed your baby before you work out so that your breasts are not as full and heavy.
- Wear a bra that supports your breasts. This will also help prevent blocked ducts.
- Avoid tight clothes that flatten your breasts.
- Be careful not to bump or bruise your breasts. Check them regularly for lumps, particularly underneath the breast and near the armpits.
- Exercises that involve lying on your stomach may be uncomfortable.
- Dancing, skipping and bike riding are all good ways to exercise.
- Take a shower afterwards, as some babies don't like the taste of sweat with their breastmilk.

Diet

You don't have to have a 'perfect' diet to be able to breastfeed. What you eat is important for your own health and energy levels, more than for your breastmilk and your baby. Even in countries where food is scarce, mothers are able to breastfeed and their babies thrive. However, there are a few nutrients a baby needs that may be affected if the mother's intake is too low, such as iodine and vitamin B_{12}.

When you are breastfeeding, your body makes up for the extra demand on nutrients by using them more efficiently. It gets some of the extra energy needed by using the fat stores laid down while you were pregnant.

Your appetite usually increases as well. You can get any extra energy and nutrients you need by eating slightly more of the same foods you would normally eat.

Iodine, iron and calcium are the nutrients of most concern in mothers who eat a normal Australian diet. Talk to your medical adviser or a dietitian to find out if you have enough of these in your diet. In the case of iodine, you are likely to be advised to take a supplement.

Thirst

Making breastmilk uses extra fluid, so breastfeeding mothers are often thirstier than usual. There are no rules about how much you need to drink. It depends on the weather conditions, your activity level and the foods you eat. Be guided by your thirst.

> Don't be tempted to ignore your thirst because you're busy. Many mothers make a habit of having a glass of water nearby each time they breastfeed their baby.

It becomes part of their breastfeeding routine. Carrying a water bottle with you when out and about also makes it easy to have a drink when you need it.

Vegetarian diets

There are two main types of vegetarian diets:
- one includes some animal products, such as dairy products and/or eggs, and in some cases fish or some other animal products
- the other does not contain any animal products (vegan).

When animal products are not eaten, or are eaten only in small amounts, your diet may be lower in protein, iron, calcium, vitamin B_{12} and omega-3 fatty acids. While you're breastfeeding, a well-planned vegetarian diet will meet these needs, with the possible exception of vitamin B_{12} in a vegan diet. If you're a long-time vegan, it would be a good idea to have your vitamin B_{12} levels checked to see if you need a supplement while you are breastfeeding.

Dairy-free diets

Dairy products are the primary source of calcium in most Australian diets. They are also a valuable source of protein and some vitamins like A, B_2 (riboflavin) and B_{12}. However, some mothers have dairy-free diets. This may be because they or their babies are intolerant to cows' milk or because dairy products are not traditional foods in their culture. When dairy products are not eaten, mothers need to get their calcium from other foods. These include canned fish with soft bones, with smaller amounts in cabbage, leeks and broccoli; nuts such as almonds and brazil nuts, and sesame seed paste (tahini). A dietitian can give personalised advice, taking into account a mother's cultural background.

Food allergy or intolerance in baby

Some babies react to traces of foods that come through their mother's breastmilk. The food allergies most commonly seen in babies are to cows' milk, eggs, peanuts and tree nuts. (The term 'tree nut' is commonly used to mean nuts such as almonds, cashews, macadamias, pecans, brazil nuts and walnuts, while peanuts are 'ground nuts'.) A baby can also have food intolerance (alone, or with an allergy) and react to a range of other foods in the mother's diet.

Babies can be unsettled for many reasons, or have other symptoms that are like those of food intolerance. Don't just assume that what you are eating is the problem. Get professional advice to help you work out whether your baby is food-sensitive. Each mother and baby pair is different. Even if you are sure that your baby is reacting to something in your diet, it can often take a long time to work out exactly which foods are causing problems. Avoiding a whole food group, such as dairy products or wheat, makes it more difficult for you to eat a balanced diet. A dietitian will be able to help you sort out what the problem foods are and ensure that your diet contains all the nutrients you need.

Mothers with medical conditions
You may have a medical condition such as coeliac disease, food allergies or another condition that requires a special diet. Breastfeeding may help protect your baby from also developing these conditions. If you are not sure if your diet is adequate, ask a dietitian for assessment and advice.

Weight loss
It's normal to store extra fat during pregnancy to provide some of the extra energy you need while breastfeeding. Mothers lose this extra weight at different times — some in the early weeks, some later and some not until after they have stopped breastfeeding. It is important that you do lose this extra weight at some point and not carry it through to another pregnancy. It is much harder to return to a healthy weight later on.

> While you're breastfeeding, it's best to lose extra weight gradually, through healthy eating and some extra exercise.

A loss of up to about half a kilo per week is safe for breastfeeding mothers. Don't use crash or fad diets, where you lose weight quickly, either during pregnancy or when breastfeeding. These diets don't have a good balance of the important nutrients you and your baby need. If you feel that you need to lose a lot of weight more quickly, consult your doctor or a dietitian for advice on a balanced weight-loss diet.

Losing too much weight
Some breastfeeding mothers have the opposite problem. They find that they lose too

much weight, too quickly. In this case, try to increase the number of serves of food you eat across all food groups. Don't be tempted to eat foods high in saturated fats or added sugar. Instead, try having frequent, small meals or eat healthy snacks between each regular meal. Consult your medical adviser or a dietitian if you are concerned about your weight loss.

Caffeine

For most of us, caffeine is part of everyday life. It's found in a wide variety of drinks, food and medication. The amount of caffeine in your breastmilk depends on how well your body absorbs and eliminates it. Caffeine levels reach their peak about 60 minutes after it's consumed. A mother can have up to three drinks a

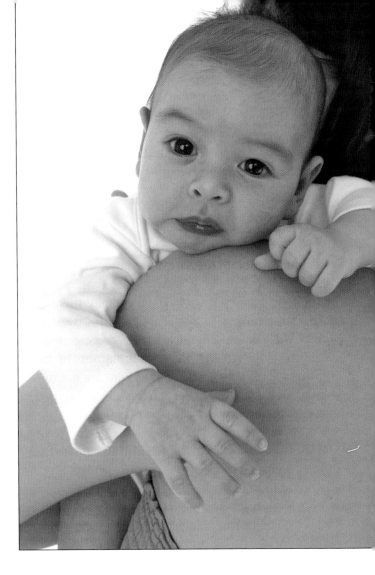

day containing caffeine without having much effect on her breastfed baby. However, avoid 'energy' drinks that contain very high amounts of caffeine and/or guarana. Knowing how caffeine affects babies can help you decide how to fit it into your diet.

- Newborns process caffeine very slowly — taking up to 80 hours to get rid of half of it. That means that the caffeine stays in their system for a long time and the level rises with each coffee or cola you drink. By the age of 6 months, the caffeine level in the baby is halved in about 2.5 hours.
- Mothers who drink a lot of strong tea, coffee or cola report a range of side effects in their babies — jitters, colic, constipation, sleep problems and unsettled behaviour.

- Caffeine can be linked to reduced milk supply, nipple vasospasm and recurrent mastitis.
- Smoking increases the effects of caffeine on breastfed babies.

When you are busy with a new baby, it can be hard to keep track of how many coffees or teas you have each day. We often grab a cuppa in place of a snack when we want a boost. Bearing in mind that caffeine is a stimulant, which affects both you and your baby, you could consider decaffeinated drinks for all but three drinks a day.

Smoking

Women who smoke during pregnancy are less likely to begin breastfeeding. If they do, they are more likely to wean earlier than non-smoking mothers. The more cigarettes a mother smokes, the less time she may spend breastfeeding.

Some smokers choose to give up breastfeeding because they are worried that their milk will contain chemicals from the cigarettes. They believe that formula-feeding may be a safer option for their babies. In fact, because of the unique protective properties of breastmilk, babies who are not breastfed are at greater risk from people smoking around them. Research shows that breastfeeding is better for a baby's health even if the mother continues to smoke.

How smoking affects babies and breastfeeding:
- Babies exposed to cigarette smoke are more likely to be hospitalised. They suffer from more respiratory and gastrointestinal illnesses, breathing problems, vomiting, eye disorders and hearing problems. They are at greater risk of SIDS.
- 'Side-stream' smoke from passive smoking is not filtered. It contains more nicotine, tar and carbon monoxide than 'mainstream' smoke drawn through the cigarette.
- Nicotine reduces appetite and can alter the taste of breastmilk. Your baby may be fussy and refuse to feed.
- When mothers smoke more than 15 cigarettes a day, babies can show signs of nicotine poisoning — vomiting after a feed, grey skin colour, loose stools, increased heart rate and restlessness. If the mother cuts back, her baby may go through withdrawal, with sleep disturbance, headaches and crying.
- Nicotine alters the make-up of breastmilk. It adds the chemical by-products of smoking and reduces vitamin levels.
- Nicotine also affects hormones. It reduces the mother's prolactin levels, which can reduce her milk supply. It also causes an adrenaline rush and this can delay the let-down reflex.

Quitting

Breastfeeding hormones may actually reduce the symptoms of nicotine withdrawal, so it may be easier to quit smoking while you are breastfeeding. Nicotine patches, if used correctly by breastfeeding mothers, reduce nicotine levels. You should be aware that the patch delivers a constant dose of nicotine to your system, so it is best to use the type of patch that you wear for only part of the day. Make sure you don't smoke any cigarettes at the same time as using a patch.

Alcohol

Under current Australian guidelines, the recommended intake of alcohol for women is no more than two standard drinks per day. However, pregnant women are advised to protect the health and development of their babies by not drinking any alcohol. Once your baby is born, you may wish to have a drink with a meal or when celebrating a special occasion. The following information may help you make informed decisions about how much and how often you drink while you are breastfeeding.

> The level of alcohol in your breastmilk is the same as the level in your blood. But breastmilk with a small amount of alcohol is still better for your baby than formula.

Alcohol will appear in your breastmilk 30–60 minutes after you start drinking. The amount of alcohol in your breastmilk will depend on:
- the strength and amount of the alcohol in your drinks
- what and how much you've eaten
- how much you weigh
- how quickly you're drinking.

How alcohol affects babies and breastfeeding:
- Depending on how often and how much you drink, alcohol can affect both breastfeeding and your baby's behaviour.
- Your milk flow may not be as strong as usual while there's alcohol in your blood. It will return to normal once your body has cleared the alcohol.
- Your baby may not sleep as well as usual. She might fall asleep more quickly, but wake sooner.
- You may not be able to take care of your baby properly if you are affected by alcohol. Arrange for someone who isn't drinking to look after her. Don't sleep

with your baby if you (or anyone else in the bed) have been drinking alcohol.
- If you regularly have three or more drinks a day, your baby may be slower to reach developmental milestones.

Planning for safe drinking:
- Time is the only thing that reduces the amount of alcohol in your breastmilk. You can't express out the 'alcoholic' milk to get rid of it, as the amount of alcohol in the new milk that replaces it will remain the same as that in your bloodstream.

As your blood alcohol level falls, so does the alcohol level in your milk. As a general rule, it takes about 2 hours for an average woman to get rid of the alcohol from 1 standard drink. That means 4 hours for 2 drinks, 6 hours for 3 drinks and so on.

- Try to avoid drinking alcohol until your baby's feeding pattern becomes fairly predictable. In the first month or so, you can't usually tell when your baby will want her next feed. This makes it difficult to plan ahead.
- Breastfeed your baby before you drink. You can then enjoy a drink knowing you probably won't need to feed again in the next couple of hours.
- Eat before and during drinking and alternate alcoholic and non-alcoholic drinks.
- If you're planning a big night (or day) where you expect to have more than 1 or 2 drinks, express some milk ahead of time. Your baby can be fed this expressed breastmilk while you wait for the alcohol to pass through your system. If you miss a feed because you are drinking, your breasts may become very full. Express to ease the discomfort and throw this milk away.

We know that not drinking alcohol is safest. Knowing the facts about how alcohol affects breastfeeding will help you decide how best to combine feeding your baby with drinking some alcohol, should you wish to do so.

You can download the free Feed Safe app for iPhone, iPad and iPod Touch (a collaboration between ABA, Reach Health Promotion Innovations and Curtin University). See feedsafe.net

Recreational drugs

It is estimated that around 1 in 4 Australian women between the ages of 14 and 39 use marijuana (cannabis), so it's worth raising the issue of its use while breastfeeding. A child's brain and nervous system develop rapidly during her first 2 years of life.

Anything that affects this growth can have long-term consequences. Chemicals from marijuana concentrate in breastmilk, so the baby gets a high dose, lasting 2–3 weeks after the mother has used marijuana. The baby may also breathe in 'side-stream' smoke. These chemicals put the baby at risk because of their effects on her growing brain. In the short-term, marijuana can make a baby sleepy, weak and feed poorly. Marijuana also affects the mother's prolactin levels and reduces milk supply. We know little about its long-term negative effects, but they are thought to be quite serious.

Prescription medications

During pregnancy and breastfeeding, your baby's health is related to your own, so it's no wonder that many mothers are concerned about taking medications. Exclusive breastfeeding is now recommended for your baby's first 6 months. Breastmilk remains her most important food for the first 12 months. In that time, even the healthiest mothers may need to take some medication. Some will need treatment for chronic medical conditions.

Breastfeeding mothers can safely use most prescribed medications
While nearly all medications enter breastmilk, most do so in amounts so low that there is no effect on the baby. Natural barriers in the cells that create breastmilk make

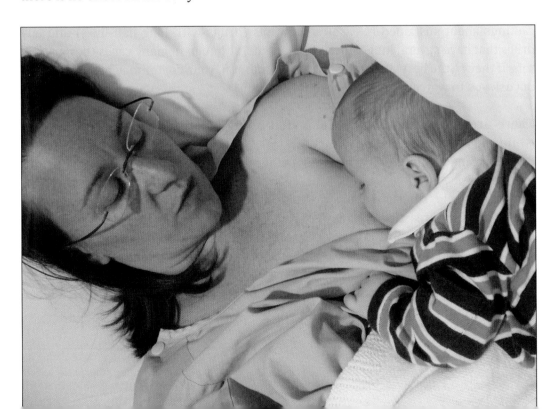

it difficult for most medications to pass into your milk. So, a very small amount of your medication reaches your baby. In general, it is considered safe if the daily dose transferred to a baby is less than 10% of the mother's dose. However, this is not the case for a small number of medications, which should not be taken while breastfeeding.

Making an informed choice

Before your doctor prescribes a medication for you, make sure he or she knows that you are breastfeeding. All drugs are divided into classes. In each class there will be a number of safe options they can choose from.

With so many new drugs available, it's often difficult for doctors to keep abreast of them all. Some choices are straightforward, but if your doctor is unsure whether or not you can breastfeed safely while taking a particular medication, ask that they check with drug information experts.

How to manage your medications

You should aim to breastfeed your baby just before you take any medication. In most cases this will mean that, by the next breastfeed, the level of the drug in your bloodstream will be low. Most drugs are absorbed into your bloodstream, rise to a peak and then drop. The faster they drop, the better for use with breastfeeding mothers.

Drugs whose levels drop quickly are said to have short half-lives. You should be cautious about sustained-release medications (drugs with long half-lives) and any drugs that have several long-acting components, although in many cases they are still safe. If they're the best choice to treat your condition, your doctor may prescribe them but ask you to watch for any effects on your baby.

There are some general principles that apply when taking any medications while you are breastfeeding:

- Take medications only when they are necessary and when the benefits outweigh the risks.
- If possible, choose medications that have been clearly proven to be the best option for breastfeeding mothers.
- Choose preparations that are non-sedating and are low in toxicity.
- If possible, avoid sustained-release medications that stay longer in your body.
- Take the medication just after a breastfeed.
- If possible, choose medications that act locally, eg ointment rather than tablets.
- Ask your doctor if there are possible effects on the baby.

Drug information services in Australia

For current information about the use of medicines/drugs during breastfeeding (or pregnancy), contact the Medicines Information Centres in your state or the NPS Medicines Line. Most of these centres operate during normal business hours.

Medicines Information Centres at hospitals
Pharmacists will answer queries on prescription and over the counter medications (eg pain relievers and cold medication), complementary medicines (eg vitamins, minerals, herbal, natural medicines), legal (eg caffeine, alcohol, nicotine) and illegal drugs (eg cannabis, heroin, ecstasy) and environmental exposure.

NPS Medicines Line
Registered nurses will answer calls in the first instance. If the query is complex, they will triage calls during business hours to specialist medicine-information pharmacists at NPS or advise the caller to see their local pharmacist or general practitioner. (NPS — Better choices, Better health: *nps.org.au*).

Caller's location	Service	Telephone (BH)
ACT	Medicines Information Centre, Canberra Hospital	02 6244 3333
NSW	MotherSafe, Royal Hospital for Women, Randwick (NSW country)	02 9382 6539 1800 647 848
QLD	NPS Medicines Line	1300 633 424
SA	Medicines Information Centre, Women's and Children's Hospital	08 8161 7222
TAS	Medicines Information Centre, Royal Hobart Hospital (Mon–Thu) NPS Medicines Line (Fri)	03 6222 8737 1300 633 424
VIC	Medicines Information Centre. Monash Medical Centre	03 9594 2361
VIC	Medicines Information Centre, Royal Women's Hospital	03 8345 3190
WA	Women & Newborn Health Services (KEMH)	08 9340 2723
All states & territories	NPS Medicines Line: *www.nps.org.au* 9 am–5 pm AEST	1300 633 424

**If your call is urgent ring the Poisons Information Centre 13 11 26
(all states & territories) 24-hours a day, 7-days a week.**

Over-the-counter remedies and herbal preparations

Before you take over-the-counter products from your health food shop or pharmacy, you should also check that they are safe. While we often assume that herbal or 'natural' remedies are harmless, this is not always true. Herbal preparations are not required to have the same level of testing and proof that they work as do prescription medicines. As a result, we know less about their side effects during breastfeeding. Some are known to be quite safe. Others have been shown to contain components that are unsafe. For instance, some herbal teas, such as chamomile, raspberry and rose hip, are considered safe during breastfeeding, while herbs such as comfrey and sassafras are not recommended. It's a good idea to do your homework before you take any herbs, especially if you are taking them at the same time as prescription medicines.

CHAPTER 11

Sex and breastfeeding

Factors related to birth

Factors related to breastfeeding

Contraception

Planning for sex

For many new parents, the title of this chapter is a contradiction in terms. Even before we become parents, our sex lives are affected by our busy work and family commitments, possible tensions in our relationships and, of course, hormones. Add a new baby, with all the extra work involved, and you may wonder how any couple ever manages to have a second child.

> **After the birth of your baby, it's natural to have fears and questions about making love. It is also natural for patterns of lovemaking to change.**

Some couples don't enjoy intercourse for at least 2 months after the birth and sometimes much longer. It depends on the amount of healing needed. Breastfeeding, rather than motherhood, is often wrongly blamed for a woman's lack of libido (interest in sex). Some people still believe that breastfeeding is 'draining' on the mother. Others think that the intense closeness a breastfeeding mother shares with her child displaces the need for closeness with her partner.

Factors related to birth

There are physical reasons why you may feel less interested in sex right now:
- You will have a vaginal discharge (lochia) for up to 6 weeks after the birth.
- You may have pain or discomfort from a vaginal tear or other damage and perhaps you have had stitches.
- You may find that your vagina is very dry so making love is painful.
- You may be exhausted. In the first weeks or months, tiredness is the most common reason for not having sex.
- Changes in body shape can also affect how sexy you feel. Your breasts, hips and thighs are most likely bigger than before. Some spreading and fanning of the outer part of your vagina after the birth is normal, too. The lips of your vagina (labia) may also seem larger and hang down further.
- Less obvious will be the change in the strength of your stomach muscles and pelvic floor. Weak stomach muscles will prevent you from fitting into figure-hugging clothes — a good diet and exercise will help you feel and look better. Weak pelvic floor muscles are no laughing matter, especially if you wet your pants when you laugh, sneeze or cough. As you get older, weak pelvic floor muscles can also cause problems with your uterus. You will enjoy sex more, be more easily aroused, and reach orgasm more often and more easily if your pelvic floor muscles are strong, so now's the time to start doing those invisible push-ups.

Factors related to breastfeeding

- Levels of two hormones — oestrogen and progesterone — rise during pregnancy and then fall rapidly after birth. Women who do not breastfeed return to their pre-pregnancy hormone levels, ovulate (produce an egg) and menstruate (have periods) within about 3 months.

Breastfeeding women generally do not regain pre-pregnancy hormone levels, ovulate or have periods until much later. The range is from about 3 months to 2 years or more. The average is around 9–10 months.

- Hormones related to breastfeeding stop the release of oestrogen and progesterone and delay the return of your fertility. How long this lasts varies from mother to mother. In rare situations, some breastfeeding women become fertile 4 weeks after delivery and a few can conceive within 12 weeks of giving birth. However, for most women, ovulation occurs much later. The length of postpartum amenorrhoea (no periods) varies widely. Many women don't have a period while their baby is exclusively breastfed.
- It is thought that low oestrogen levels make the vaginal wall thinner, less elastic and less lubricated. After giving birth, many mothers find they need to use a lubricant for a while.
- Some people find full or leaking breasts can be uncomfortable or off-putting during sex. For others, it is a real turn-on. It is common for milk to leak from the breasts during arousal just as it is common to feel mild sexual arousal when your baby breastfeeds. This is because the same hormone — oxytocin — triggers both the let-down reflex and orgasm. There is no need to feel guilty. Any good feelings that encourage breastfeeding are to a baby's advantage.

Psychological factors:
- Pain, fatigue and hormones all affect your emotions at this time.
- You may fear that having sex will be painful.
- You may worry that you'll get pregnant again before you are ready.
- You may believe that your partner won't find your new body attractive.
- You may not want to 'share' your body with your partner now that your baby seems to have first claim on it. Nearly all mothers feel 'touched out' at some time.
- You may be feeling anxious about money, especially if your family income has been reduced.

Contraception

Research studies have shown that you are 98% protected against pregnancy for up to 6 months after your baby's birth if all the following are true for you:

- You are fully (or almost fully) breastfeeding. This means that you are not giving your child formula, other fluids or solids on a regular basis.
- Your baby is feeding often, day and night, with no long breaks in between.
- You have not had a period since giving birth.

The most widely-used contraceptives for breastfeeding mothers are:

- The progesterone-only ones ('mini-pill', progesterone-only injections and implants). However, be aware that the 'mini-pill' frequently prescribed for breastfeeding women has been shown to affect the milk supply for some.
- The intrauterine device (IUD), the diaphragm, condoms and spermicides.
- Ovulation awareness methods, such as the Billings Method.

The combined oral contraceptive pill is not recommended for breastfeeding mothers. It has been shown to reduce milk supply because it contains oestrogen. Consult your medical adviser about any oral or injected forms of contraception. A family planning doctor will be able to help you decide what is best for you.

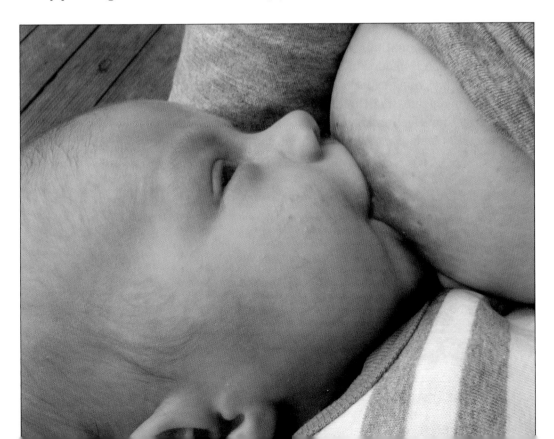

Planning for sex

Once you become parents, sex rarely 'just happens'. Mostly you need to plan for it. This might mean planning to make love at 7 pm, if your baby has just fallen asleep, rather than sitting up watching television and going into bed at 11 pm, when the baby is likely to wake. Remember how creative you had to be when you first got together if you had nowhere private to kiss and cuddle? Now may be a good time to revive some of those exciting times. Sex can happen in places other than your bed.

Lots of partners expect that their sex life will go back to normal once they get the all clear at the 6-week check-up. If this doesn't happen and the weeks go by with no hint of romance in the air, many relationships start to feel the strain. Don't assume that you are the only ones going through this. Your friends may or may not tell you that they still don't feel like having sex. Men are even less likely to tell their mates the truth. Unless someone knows what it's like to spend most of each day and night physically attached to a little baby, it can be almost impossible to understand just how this affects you. Let your partner know how you feel, physically and emotionally.

If your breasts are sore, or your vagina is dry, say so. If you don't feel like sex, but would love a cuddle, say so. If you had a good night's rest and found yourself fantasising about sex while you were doing the dishes, say so. Even if you don't have intercourse, it will help both of you to realise that you are still sexual people and that there are many ways of relating sexually. Loving each other does not have to be restricted to having sex. Touching, bathing together, or those three important words 'I love you' are sometimes all that is needed to create closeness.

Take your time, don't expect too much of yourselves and be reassured that your sex life will resume in due time. However, this does mean that you need to understand and accept each other's feelings. If you and your partner are out of balance with each other regarding sex or feeling angry and resentful, you might think about seeking professional help.

Time, patience and good communication will help you to get back 'in tune' with each other.

CHAPTER 12

Asleep and awake

Some facts about sleep
and babies

Getting your baby to sleep

Co-sleeping

Safe sleeping with your baby
— some dos and don'ts

'Controlled crying'

Sleeping, or more correctly the lack of it, is a big issue for most parents. Perhaps this is because in our culture babies are still expected to fit in with adults rather than the other way round. Sadly, sleep sometimes becomes a battle between parent and baby, one which parents are expected to win at all costs.

The issue is that your baby's sleep patterns do not match yours. Often, it is a matter of coming to terms with the reality of babies compared to the fantasy.

Some facts about sleep and babies

- It's healthy and normal for babies and young children to wake during the night and to need attention and comfort from their parents.
- Frequent waking is essential to babies' growth. It's a survival mechanism to make sure they get enough food to grow.
- Most babies take quite a while to form their own sleep routine and to sleep for lengthy periods. Sleeping and waking varies widely from baby to baby just as it does in older children and adults. Many adults don't sleep through the night either.
- 'Sleeping through' for a baby is defined as 5 hours, not the 8 hours we think of as a good night's sleep for adults.
- Babies whose parents respond to their crying promptly settle better in the long term because they know that their needs are understood and will be met.
- Crying is a sign of distress or discomfort, not that your baby is spoilt or 'naughty'.
- Every baby is aware of the presence (or absence) of her chief source of comfort and security — her parents. If you're out of sight, she has no way of knowing when or if you will return.
- Babies have no control over their sleeping.
- A baby's sleep patterns are different from an adult's. There are two basic types of sleep — quiet sleep, when the breathing is slow and regular and the body hardly moves, and active sleep, when breathing is faster and uneven and there are lots of body and facial movements. Very young babies usually sleep a lot as they need to conserve energy to grow. About 60% of this is Rapid Eye Movement (REM) sleep, the more active sleep. New babies spend about twice as much time as adults in active sleep. As your baby grows, and her brain matures, the amount of REM sleep decreases to 20%. Large amounts of REM may be important to help the brain develop.
- Frequent arousals, where the baby nearly wakes up, play a part in protecting a baby against SIDS.

- Some parents try to get their baby to sleep longer at night by cutting short the daytime sleeps or keeping the baby up later so that she is more tired. However, these often result in an over-tired baby, an even more disturbed night and an unhappy baby the next day. Babies usually sleep better at night if they have had a good sleep during the day.
- Despite what many people will tell you, research shows that mothers of formula-fed babies don't get any more sleep than breastfeeding mothers. In fact, breastfeeding mothers get more.
- Wakeful babies usually reach their developmental milestones sooner because they tend to interact more with their parents.

Getting your baby to sleep

Sleeping and eating are two things that you should not force your baby to do. It takes time, patience and being willing to go with the flow before you can reach a balance between your babies' sleeping needs and your own.

Most babies feed to sleep. Although this seems to be frowned upon by some, there is physiological evidence that this is normal.

A hormone, called cholecystokinin (CCK) is released in both mother and baby at the end of a feed. This makes both feel sleepy. In the baby, this hormone peaks at the end of a feed, drops and then peaks again 30–60+ minutes later. This later peak is thought to be caused by the breastmilk, especially the fat, in the baby's stomach. So the baby sucks, dozes off and may wake again shortly, perhaps for a short top-up feed, before going into a deeper sleep.

Some other ways of helping your baby sleep:
- Rock your baby or carry her in a sling. The motion, warmth and comfort of your body often help your baby drop off to sleep. Dads are usually fantastic at rocking. They seem to have the knack of getting the tempo and motion just right.
- A walk in the stroller or pram sometimes works, although many babies usually wake once the motion stops.
- Background noise is helpful. Hum or sing a favourite song over and over, put on some soothing music or rock your baby to a definite rhythm.
- Many babies like to be lightly swaddled when put down to sleep alone, especially when on their backs, as is recommended. Babies have a natural startle response

when lowered backwards or even when lying still on their backs. Their arms fling outwards and they seem frightened of falling. Swaddling can make them feel more secure. Use a light, open-weave fabric so your baby doesn't get too hot.

Some ideas for coping with a wakeful baby:
- Try to remain calm.
- Try to arrange time for yourself so you can catch up on sleep, perhaps taking it in turns with your partner to go to bed early.
- Eat well.
- Seek support from people you know will be sympathetic. Accept any help you can get with other chores.
- Reduce other stresses in your life as much as you can.
- If you are feeling so frustrated with your baby to the point that you fear that you may harm her, leave her safely in her cot for a few minutes and go out of the room. A few minutes crying alone is less harmful to her than you not being able to control your emotions.
- You may have to give up some of your evening adult time to get a couple of extra hours sleep once your baby goes to sleep. Daytime naps can also make a big difference. A well rested mother is better than a sparkling clean house.
- Avoid interruptions to your sleep times. Why not put a note on your door saying, 'Mum and baby sleeping. Please call back later' or take your phone off the hook or put your mobile on silent? If you tell your family and friends that, if you don't answer, you are probably asleep they won't be concerned if you're out of contact for a couple of hours.
- If you are feeling pressured by other people's expectations and opinions, a little white lie may be in order. Just nod and smile to questions about whether she is a good sleeper. For a baby, she probably is.

A checklist of reasons for frequent waking

There are a number of common (and normal) reasons why babies wake. As she grows, her reasons for waking may change. Your response to her waking will also change.

- **Is it your first week at home?** After a sleepy period straight after birth, newborn babies can be unsettled for the next few days and after they arrive home. One of the reasons is that colostrum contains apomorphine that helps babies sleep to conserve energy. This effect wears off once the baby graduates to mature breastmilk. Time, a relaxed attitude and patience help your baby adjust.
- **Could your baby be hungry?** If your baby wakes 1–2 hours after her last feed, she is probably hungry. Feeding is usually the quickest and most effective remedy.
- **Is she uncomfortable?** Perhaps she is too hot, too cold, needs a nappy change, or would prefer to be more or less snugly wrapped. Perhaps she has been woken by a sudden sound and is frightened. Babies who sleep through daytime noise may become unsettled when the house is quiet.
- **Is she lonely?** Babies are reassured by physical contact and may prefer to see you or be near you. Trying to teach her a lesson by not giving her comfort will only make a sensitive baby more insecure.
- **Is she unwell?** A sudden change to your baby's feeding and sleeping habits may mean that she is ill. If medication is prescribed, ask whether it affects sleep.
- **Could it be something you ate?** Some breastfed babies react when their mothers eat or drink certain foods or medication. Discuss this with your medical adviser.
- **Is she teething?** If your baby seems upset, is drooling, has slight cold symptoms, seems to want to chew often and has swollen gums, she may well be teething. Babies can have teething symptoms for weeks before the teeth actually appear.

Co-sleeping

Most babies feel safer — and so sleep better — when they are close to their parents. With your baby nearby, you can also respond to her cues quickly. She is able to breastfeed whenever she needs without disturbing you to the point where you're wide awake. So you'll both quickly settle back to sleep.

Quite often there is a fear that once your baby begins to sleep with (or near) you, she will be dependent on you forever. However, if you can be relaxed about her presence, she will soon feel more secure and able to sleep on her own. You can wait until she is a little older and naturally ready to move into her own bed. Or you can help her make the transition earlier if you prefer.

There are many options available for keeping your baby close to you at sleeptime. She can sleep in the same bed as you; next to your bed on a separate sleep surface; or with her cot close to your bed so she can see and hear you.

Safe sleeping with your baby — some dos and don'ts

It is not safe to share a bed with your baby:
- If you or your partner:
  - o are a smoker or if the mother smoked during pregnancy (no matter how often, what, where or when you smoked),
    have consumed any alcohol or taken illegal or sleep-inducing drugs,
  - o are unusually tired, to a point where you would find it hard to respond to your baby.
- In the early months, if your baby was born very small or premature.
- If your baby is formula-fed, it may be safer for your baby to sleep in a cot in your room.

In addition:
- Don't sleep with your baby on a sofa, waterbed, armchair, bean bag etc.
- Don't let your baby sleep alone in a bed, on a sofa, bean bag etc.
- Don't let other children sleep next to your baby.
- Don't let pets share a bed with your baby, or leave a baby alone in a room that pets can get to.

If sharing a bed with your baby:
- Put your baby on his back to sleep, never on his front or side.
- Make sure your baby cannot fall out of bed or get stuck between the mattress and a wall or furniture.
- Make sure the bedclothes or bedding cannot cover your baby's face.
- Don't overdress your baby or cover his head.
- Your baby should not wear a sleeping bag as well as being under the covers.
- Don't swaddle your baby.
- Don't use an electric blanket on a bed where your baby is sleeping.
- Whenever possible, use natural fibres that allow for better air flow.
- The mattress should be firm, flat, clean, and not smell of chemicals. Do not dry-clean bedding.
- Make sure your partner knows that your baby is in the bed.

If you are unable to provide a safe sleeping environment for your baby in your bed, having your baby sleep in a cot in the same room is a safer alternative.

'Controlled crying'

Some people, including health professionals, will advise you to use 'controlled crying'. Also known as controlled comforting, sleep training or self-settling, this is when you let your baby 'cry it out' in the hope that she will learn to go back to sleep by herself.

Keep in mind, though, that crying is your baby's means of communicating distress. She is not crying to annoy you. Meeting her needs will not 'spoil' her. On the contrary, she will learn more quickly how to tell you what she wants and that the world is a secure and loving place. Without you to come to her aid when she cries, she is helpless.

Before you decide to let her 'cry it out', consider these questions. Is there an obvious reason for her crying? How do you feel about listening to it? How important is it to you to comfort your baby when she is scared or lonely? If you ignore her cries, will it solve or worsen the problem?

Given that sleep training programs have become so common that many parents have come to believe they must enrol in 'sleep school', it is worth noting the evidence-based opinion of the Australian Association of Infant Mental Health (AAIMHI). It has position statements on its website at: *aaimhi.org>policies & submissions*, in particular *Position Statement 1: Controlled Crying* (October 2013) and *Position Statement 2: Responding to Infant Cues* (September 2006). These statements can be downloaded as PDFs from this website. You might like to read these position statements in full before you make your decisions on this issue.

The first statement from AAIMHI includes:
> *AAIMHI is concerned that the widely practiced technique of controlled crying is not consistent with infants' and toddlers' needs for optimal emotional and psychological health and may have unintended negative consequences.* AAIMHI 2013

And from the second statement:
> *... it is now wrong to advise parents that routinely refusing attention to a crying baby will bring no harm... Babies become distressed if left to cry alone, and this can precipitate negative long term psychological consequences if done repeatedly.* AAIMHI 2006

CHAPTER 13

A question of supply

Do you really have a low supply?

Reasons for low supply

How to make more milk

Too much milk

Most new mothers worry about whether they will have enough breastmilk. However, supply is rarely a problem if you understand the principle of supply and demand. This controls how much breastmilk you can make.

Do you really have a low supply?

In most cases the real problem is that mothers don't know how to tell if their baby is getting enough breastmilk. The checklist in Chapter 6 is a good guide. Many mothers are not confident that they can provide enough breastmilk and worry when their babies seem unsettled. Often, they do not pick up normal infant cues where the baby is telling them they need a breastfeed. Here is a list of times when mothers often wrongly think that there is a drop in their milk supply:

- When the early engorged feeling passes and your breasts become softer as your milk supply settles down to match your baby's needs.
- When your baby needs more feeds than in the first days or weeks.
- When your baby grows stronger and becomes expert at emptying the breast — often in just a few minutes. It can be hard to believe he can now take a full feed so quickly.
- In later months when you find your breasts are smaller.
- When your baby is older and you may not feel your let-down any more.
- When the weather is hot and your baby is feeding more often to quench his thirst.
- When your baby has a few fussy or 'hungry' days and wants to breastfeed more often than usual. It used to be thought that the baby was having an 'appetite increase' or 'growth spurt', where he needed more milk to meet his growing needs. However, we now know that a baby's daily intake remains about the same from 1–6 months of age. It is now thought that these fussy times are related to big steps forward in the baby's mental development. Some people call these 'wonder weeks'. If you follow your baby's lead and breastfeed more often for a few days, you will probably find that he soon settles down again. The comfort he receives from these extra breastfeeds also plays an important role in his development.
- When your baby is unsettled even after being allowed to breastfeed for as long as he wants. Simple discomfort or even illness (an ear infection, thrush, teething) could be the cause.
- When your baby has more than 10 wet and many dirty nappies each day, and is continually unsettled and perhaps even colicky. People often think this is because they don't have enough milk, when it's usually a case of too much.
- When a baby who has gained large amounts of weight in the early weeks

(common in breastfed babies) suddenly changes to a slower gaining pattern, or a large baby's weight gain slows temporarily. It is common for weight gains to slow down between 3–6 months.

If you have ruled out all these and you are still concerned, it's worth talking things over with a breastfeeding counsellor. She can help you firstly work out if you have a problem, and secondly if it's a breastfeeding management problem. You might also consider seeing a lactation consultant or your doctor who can check whether there are any anatomical problems affecting your baby's sucking. There are some (very rare) conditions that can prevent a baby from making the best use of breastmilk, or stop a baby from sucking well. More often than not the problem turns out to be unrelated to milk supply.

Reasons for low supply

Getting the supply-and-demand balance right is a matter of give and take. You and your baby need to work together. A number of factors may prevent you from doing so.

Feeding factors:
- **Too-few feeds, too-short feeds.** The more milk he removes from the breast, the more milk you will make. A baby who is fed on a schedule may not be telling the breasts to make enough milk.
- **Changing sides after a set time,** rather than watching for signs that he has had enough from the first breast. It is your baby who drives your milk supply, so he needs to feed for as long as he wants on each side. He has had enough when his sucking slows, or he lets go or falls asleep.
- **Poor attachment or sucking technique** of the baby at the breast. A baby who cannot milk the breast well may not take enough of the milk available in the breast. This means he will have less fluid, fewer wet nappies, slower weight gains. Your supply will drop and you may have sore nipples. This is more common with weak, sick or sleepy newborn babies if they are not put to the breast early and often. Sometimes, the baby does not have to work for the milk because of a strong let-down reflex or oversupply. It may also happen if your baby has been confused about how to suck at the breast because he has been given bottles or dummies in the early days.
- **If you wait until your baby is crying before feeding him,** he won't feed as well. Offer the breast as soon as he starts to stir and is still calm, so he will take a good feed.

- **Regular use of complementary feeds** — if you have been regularly using infant formula when leaving your baby, or to 'top up' after breastfeeds — will reduce your baby's demand for breastmilk and so reduce your supply.
- **If solids or fruit juices are given too soon**, your baby will ask for less breastmilk and your supply will drop. Breastmilk alone is the only food that your baby needs for about the first 6 months. It is also the most nutritious. *All other foods are inferior and less suited to your baby's digestive system.*
- **Mothers who return to work or study outside of the home** sometimes notice a drop in their milk supply if they use infant formula to complement or replace expressed breastmilk. More frequent feeds in the evenings and/or at weekends can overcome this.

Mother-centred factors:
- **During ovulation or your period,** the balance of hormones in your body changes and your baby may not feed as well for a time. Don't worry, he will usually make up for it when your hormones settle down again.
- **The use of a hormonal form of contraception,** containing oestrogen (ie the

'Pill'), may cause your milk supply to drop. Breastfeeding mothers are usually only prescribed the progesterone-based contraceptives (the 'mini-pill'). However, some mothers have reported that even these have caused their babies to be fussy. Frequent feeding is usually enough to offset this. If not, you may need to discuss other methods of contraception.

- **If you become pregnant,** your supply may decrease and your baby may fuss at the breast. Some mothers prefer to wean at this time. However, others continue to breastfeed. For more information, read the article *Breastfeeding through pregnancy and beyond* on the ABA website.
- **Some drugs, both prescribed and over-the-counter,** can affect breastfeeding. They may pass through the milk to your baby or affect your milk supply. Make sure you tell your doctor or pharmacist that you are breastfeeding and discuss the effects of any medication you are prescribed.
- **Excessive amounts of alcohol, nicotine and caffeine** (in tea, coffee, cola drinks, chocolate etc) may affect the let-down reflex and the production of milk. They may make your baby irritable or restless. Try to limit these while you are breastfeeding. See Chapter 10 for more details.
- **If you have been ill or have had surgery,** your milk supply may be lower. A bout of mastitis can also cause a sudden decrease in supply in the affected breast. Rest and feed your baby frequently, both during your illness and after, to increase your milk supply again.
- **There may be physical reasons** why a mother is not able to produce enough milk for her baby. A very small number of women do not have enough glandular tissue; some have hormonal problems or a retained placenta following the birth, while others have had previous breast surgery. These factors can all affect how much milk they can produce.

How to make more milk

Remember: supply equals demand. To make more milk, your baby (or you, via expressing) needs to remove the milk that is made.

- **Make sure your baby is attached well and is feeding often.** To maintain their supply, most mothers need to feed at least 8–12 times or more in 24 hours. Not every feed will be of the same length. Some may just be a quick snack while others may be long and leisurely and take a half hour or so. Try offering the breast more often than usual for several days.

- **Go with the flow.** If your baby is hungrier and wants to feed more often, let him do so. This is nature's way of making sure you continue to make enough milk to match his needs.
- **Allow your baby to have skin-to-skin contact with you.** It will help him relax and will also boost your hormone levels to help you make more milk.
- **Expressing, either by hand or pump, after a breastfeed** will also help to remove more milk so the breast will make more to replace it.
- **Try stroking the breast towards the nipple** on all sides as your baby feeds. Or use 'breast compression'. Compress your breast with your spare hand while your baby feeds. You may notice he drinks more when you do that. Keep the pressure on your breast until his swallowing slows again and then squeeze a different part of your breast. Take care not to pull the nipple from his mouth.
- **Change sides several times during a feed** if your baby is sleepy and dozes off at the breast after only a few minutes or whenever his sucking slows. This will help him to suck more strongly and so trigger more let-downs. Wake and burp your baby as you switch sides to get the greatest amount of milk into him in the least amount of time, before he gets too sleepy to feed more.
- **Offer little breastmilk 'snack' feeds when your baby is awake.**
- **Offer the breast as a comforter** for a few days instead of a dummy.
- **Rest whenever you are able and try to eat well.** Do your best not to become stressed. Your health and wellbeing are important.
- **Avoid giving water, juice or any other foods,** unless there is a clear medical reason. These will lessen your baby's interest in breastfeeding and your supply will drop. On the other hand, he needs energy to feed well, so he may do better if he has a calorie boost. This is the time to use your store of expressed breastmilk, if you have one, or you may wish to express between feeds and give the collected milk as a top-up after the next feed. Occasionally complementary formula may be necessary for a short time. In such cases, with support and information from an ABA counsellor, you can boost your supply and return to full breastfeeding. Mothers who have weaned their babies have also been able to return to full breastfeeding.
- **A breastfeeding supplementer** may help build up a low supply. This allows the baby to feed at the breast and get either expressed breastmilk or infant formula from a tube at the same time. A special container is worn around your neck. Fine tubing carries expressed breastmilk or formula from the container to the nipple. When your baby suckles the breast, milk is drawn through the tube into his mouth along with milk directly from the breast. Cleaning the supplementer is time-consuming and some women find it awkward to use.

However, it can be invaluable because it encourages a baby to suckle while his mother rebuilds her supply.

- **There are medications (both prescription and herbal preparations)** which are sometimes prescribed by health professionals for the small group of mothers who struggle to produce enough milk. Substances that are claimed to increase milk supply are known as galactagogues. The most common drug used in Australia to treat medically-diagnosed low supply is domperidone. Like any drug, there are side effects so the benefits have to be weighed against these. There are also side effects to plants and medicinal herbs (such as fenugreek) commonly recommended to increase milk supply. Galactagogues, whether or not they produce an effect, are not a replacement for the basic breastfeeding methods of increasing supply detailed above.

Too much milk

While many mothers worry about whether they have enough milk for their babies, there are also some who have too much milk. It usually takes at least 6 weeks for your breasts to adjust to making just the right amount of milk for your baby at each feed. Occasionally a mother can have problems with too much milk past that time.

You may be making too much milk if:
- Your breasts seem to fill quickly.
- Your breasts are often lumpy and tight, despite softening with a breastfeed.
- Your baby gags, gulps (especially at the start of a feed) and often will not take the second breast.
- Your baby may bring up quite a lot of milk at the end of the feed.
- Often, baby gains a lot of weight quickly; but very occasionally poor weight gain can occur.
- Your baby may be extra fussy between feeds, especially in the evening.
- You are changing lots of wet nappies (ie more than the usual 5 heavy wet disposable nappies or 6–8 heavy wet cloth nappies in 24 hours).
- Your baby generally has a bowel motion at each feed that is often green and frothy (and possibly also explosive).

Managing an oversupply
If you continue to have too much milk, there are several things you can do to reduce your supply.

- **Feed only from one breast at each feed.** Allow your baby to feed for as long as he needs on that breast. It may take him up to 30 minutes to get as much milk as he wants following the initial fast flow. Once your supply adjusts, you may be able to go back to offering both breasts at each feed. If your other breast feels full and hard, particularly at the early morning feed, you may need to gently express just enough to make yourself comfortable.
- **Feeding from the one breast for two or more feeds in a row** may help fix the problem of oversupply. This is called 'block-feeding'. Choose a block of time, say 4 hours. Each time during that block your baby wants to feed, you offer the same breast. In the next 4-hour block, you only offer the other breast. How long you make the block depends on the degree of your oversupply. It usually takes 3–4 days for this to have an effect. Keep an eye on your baby's wet and dirty nappies. Go back to a normal feeding pattern when your supply settles down. You always need to make sure that the unused breast isn't too full and that there are no signs of blocked ducts or hard areas in the breast. If these develop, clear them straight away either by feeding or expressing.
- It can also be helpful to:
  - Express only when necessary for your comfort or to help your baby attach properly if your breast is too full or hard.
  - Limit the amount of comfort sucking by using other soothing techniques such as rocking or a dummy.
  - Avoid giving your baby extra fluids or solids as this may make your supply problems worse.
  - Check your breasts each day for signs of tightness or lumps. Massage or express lumps until they soften.
  - Use cold packs between feeds to make your breasts feel more comfortable.

A forceful let-down and fast flow

Sometimes, too much milk leads to a very strong let-down reflex and fast flow of milk. Your milk sprays out from both breasts, making your baby gag, splutter and sometimes pull away as your milk lets down. He may cry and fight the breast and may seem colicky and unsettled, especially in the early evening. He will often have a bowel motion after each feed and this may be green and frothy. He may bring up small amounts of milk after or between feeds, usually with a burp.

It should be noted, however, that this is not always associated with an oversupply. Some mothers with normal supply have a very strong let-down and fast flow. Their babies may gulp and gag at the beginning of a feed, but will settle as the feed progresses. Their weight gains will be adequate.

If your let-down and milk flow are a problem for your baby, there are a number of ideas that you can try:

- **Trigger your let-down reflex** by hand before you put your baby to the breast, catching the first flow of milk in a nappy or cloth. This will help save your baby from being swamped with milk and encourage him to feed and empty the breast.
- **Try feeding your baby while reclining back** with your baby on your tummy so that he is effectively sucking uphill. This may help him cope with the fast flow of milk. Make sure he is attached well, as this can be tricky in unusual positions. Some mothers find that just lying down to feed (both mother and baby on their sides) helps slow the flow a little.
- **Burp your baby after 3–4 minutes** if you need to and then put him back to finish his feed from that side. This can help to prevent wind problems.
- **Pay more attention to burping your baby after he finishes each side.** Putting gentle pressure on his tummy can help expel air bubbles. If you think he is uncomfortable, rubbing his tummy or lower back with massage oil can help, as can rocking him or giving him a warm bath.
- **Persevere.** You may need to try these suggestions or a combination of them for a few days before you notice any real change.

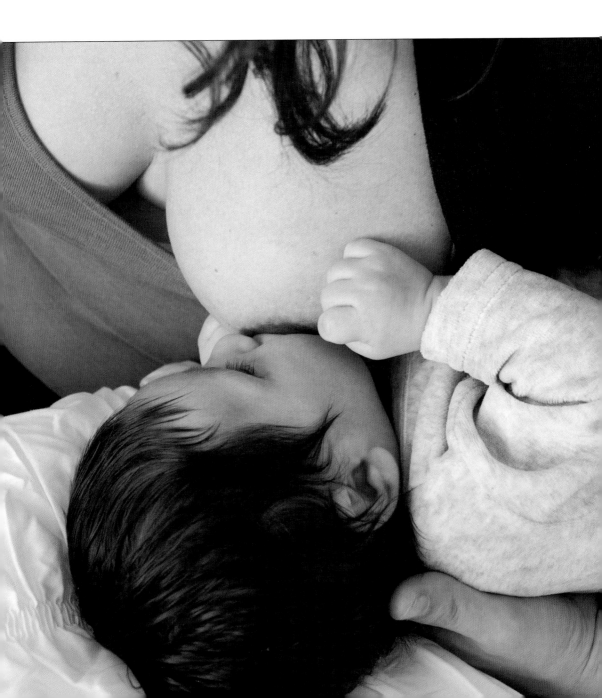

CHAPTER 14

Common breastfeeding challenges

Sore nipples

Cracked nipples

Blocked duct

Mastitis

Breast abscess

Having accurate information will prevent a lot of common breastfeeding problems. Sometimes though, even with the best care, things can go wrong. The sooner you ask for help, the quicker the problem can be resolved. Start by reading this chapter and then calling the Breastfeeding Helpline on 1800 686 268 if you need to.

If your breasts or nipples are tender or painful, or if feeding your baby has become an endurance test rather than an enjoyable experience, you may be wondering whether it is all worth it. Often weaning is seen as a quick fix and mothers may be told it is the only option. However, most women look back with regret if they weaned before they started enjoying their breastfeeding relationship. **In most cases weaning is not the best solution.**

Sore nipples

The most common reason for sore and damaged nipples is the baby's poor attachment to the breast.

It can take a little while to get used to the strong sucking of a healthy baby. When you begin breastfeeding, your nipples will be sensitive and many mothers experience some early nipple pain with initial attachment. You'll be pleased to know that, for most mothers, sore nipples cease to be a problem after the first week or so.

Taking care in getting your baby on and off your breast, some simple first-aid treatment, and a little time and patience are usually all that is needed to solve the problem. You will find that sore nipples improve quickly once you learn how to attach your baby correctly. Doing baby-led attachment (see Chapter 5) with your baby often, particularly in the early weeks, can help get breastfeeding working well for you and your baby.

First aid for sore nipples and how to avoid soreness:
- **Feed frequently.**
- **Don't wait until your baby is crying.** If she is calmer when she comes to the breast, it will be easier to attach her and she will suck more gently.
- **Trigger your let-down before you attach your baby.** If your nipples hurt most at the beginning of a feed, before your milk lets down, gently massage your breast and express some milk beforehand. This starts the milk flowing. It softens the areola so that your nipple is easier for your baby to grasp. The milk lubricates your nipple so that it slides more easily into her mouth.
- **Relax and consider pain medication**. If you find yourself dreading each feed,

try to relax and breathe deeply to help you cope with the pain. Simple pain relieving medication like paracetamol may help.

- **Make sure your baby is positioned to attach well.** Remember to bring your baby to your breast rather than moving forward to put your nipple into her mouth. Once she is attached properly and the milk starts flowing, any pain usually disappears. If it doesn't, check her attachment. You may need to take her off the breast and start the feed again.
- **Take care if you need to re-attach.** First break the suction so you don't do more damage. You can do this by putting a (clean) finger into the corner of her mouth before taking her off.
- **Feed from the less sore side first.** This will take the edge off your baby's hunger and make sure your milk is flowing freely when she attaches to the sore nipple.
- **Check your nipples after each feed.** You may notice a line of swelling and redness across it. There may be a white area or even a small stripe of blood under the skin, or the nipple may look squashed or ridged as it comes out of her mouth. These are signs that your nipple is stressed by your baby's sucking and that you need to work to improve her attachment.
- **Try different feeding positions.** Changing her position for part of the feed may help. Use the twin position, holding your baby under your arm and against your body on the side from which she is feeding. Her head should face your nipple with her feet behind you. Try feeding in bed, with both of you lying on your sides and facing each other. You need to check that your nipple and a good portion of the underside of your areola are well into her mouth. Her chin should be pressed into your breast and her lips turned out.
- **Use a pillow to bring your baby level with your breasts.** Your baby's mouth should be level with the natural height of your nipple, so that you are not lifting your breast to her level. While she is small, it may help to support her with extra pillows. This helps keep the nipple in her mouth and prevents her pulling back and stretching it. Do not raise your baby's body too high.
- **Limit comfort sucking after your baby has fed.** Most babies like to stay at the breast for extra sucking after they have taken most of the milk. This relaxes and comforts them and helps them settle. They also get more of the very nourishing hindmilk. If your nipples are sore, you can shorten your baby's comfort sucking time. Let her satisfy this need by sucking on your finger or a dummy. You can also try rocking, cuddling and patting her. If this does not work, another short feed half an hour or so later will probably settle her.
- **Take care of your nipple skin.** Avoid using soaps, shampoos or harsh towels on your nipples as they may damage the delicate skin. Make sure your bras fit

well and avoid nursing pads that hold moisture against the skin. Be careful in both your choice and use of breast pumps. If you need to use a nipple shield in the short-term, make sure you do so with the assistance of a breastfeeding counsellor or lactation consultant.

- **Rub some breastmilk on your nipples after each feed.** Breastmilk has anti-infective and healing properties. Express a few drops at the end of the feed and smear the milk over your nipple and let it dry thoroughly. There is no need to wash your nipples before and after each feed as this can dry the skin. It's best to leave the natural oils to do their job. Specially designed breast shells or nipple protectors can be worn inside your bra. They allow air to circulate around your nipples and stop clothing from rubbing them.

- **Be cautious about using nipple creams.** Most breastfeeding authorities advise that nipple creams are unnecessary unless prescribed for a specific medical condition. Creams and other preparations sometimes worsen rather than cure problems. They can affect the skin and also harbour germs and other organisms such as thrush. A few drops of breastmilk smeared over your nipples can be the best nipple cream.

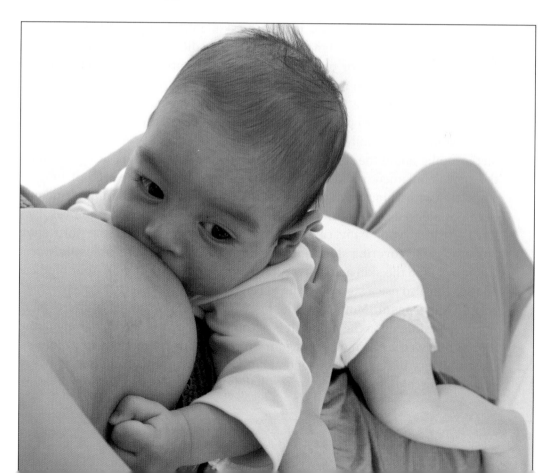

- **Watch out for potential problems as your baby grows.** Although nipple pain is most common in the early weeks, it can recur when your baby is older.
  - Heavy babies held loosely on the lap may drag on the nipples.
  - Acrobatic and inquisitive older babies may turn and twist at the breast without letting go, stretching the nipple.
  - Babies who sleep at the breast and hold onto the nipple sometimes bite to catch it if they feel it sliding out.
  - Teething babies can sometimes bite to relieve their sore gums. Give your baby something hard and cold to chew on before a feed. Some mothers feel that changes to their babies' saliva during teething can irritate their nipples. Try rinsing the nipple area with a little bicarbonate of soda dissolved in water (about 1 teaspoon to 1 cup).
  - Hormonal changes associated with menstruation, ovulation or pregnancy can also cause nipple tenderness.

Medical reasons for sore nipples:
- **Dermatitis or infection.** If your nipples suddenly become very sore when feeding an older baby, you should consult your medical adviser. If your nipples are red, itchy or sore to the touch, or if the skin on the nipple and areola looks scaly or flaky, it may be a sign that there is a medical problem. You may have dermatitis, or a thrush or bacterial infection. Dermatitis can be caused by an allergic reaction to a nipple cream or soaps, shampoos or detergent residues in clothing. Stop using the suspect substances until you sort out the cause. Try washing your bras with pure soap, rinse well and dry in the sun.
- **White spot.** Occasionally, a tiny white blister (called 'white spot') may appear on the nipple, about the size of a pin-head or a little larger. Often the area around the spot is inflamed, red and painful, usually throughout the feed. It may be associated with a blocked duct and mastitis, and occurs when the nipple opening becomes blocked by skin or a plug of milk. It is fairly rare and often resolves itself. Position your baby carefully to minimise pressure on the sore spot. Sometimes the covering skin can be removed by soaking your breast in warm water to soften the skin and allow you to express the plug of milk. Your medical adviser can also use a sterile needle to remove the plug if necessary.
- **Nipple vasospasm.** Mothers with this condition complain of a sharp pain, burning or stinging in the nipple. It is accompanied by sudden whitening of the nipple, followed by a colour change from red to blue. In many cases, mothers have a history of Raynaud's phenomenon. People with this condition are very sensitive to cold, particularly in the hands and feet. If it only occurs when

breastfeeding, nipple vasospasm is most likely a sign that incorrect attachment is stressing and damaging the nipples. It can also occur when there is an infection on the nipples. If the underlying causes are treated, the vasospasm should stop. If it occurs between feeds, keeping your breasts warm and applying some extra warmth to the affected area may help relieve the symptoms.

Cracked nipples

Properly managed, sore nipples usually improve quickly. However, if they are left untreated, they can develop fissures (or cracks) in the skin. Sometimes you can see the crack on the tip of the nipple or where the nipple joins the areola, but sometimes it is too fine to be seen easily. Feeding is usually very painful and may even cause bleeding. Although bleeding may look alarming and blood may even show up in your baby's bowel motions or regurgitated milk, it won't harm her. It is quite safe to keep breastfeeding. Too much blood in the feed may irritate the stomach, causing the baby to vomit, but this is still not harmful to the baby.

In most cases, cracked nipples are the result of incorrect positioning and attachment. They heal quickly once this is fixed. Other possible causes are:
- medical conditions such as thrush, bacterial infection or dermatitis
- incorrect use of breast pumps
- tongue-tie
- shape of your baby's mouth.

If you are concerned, ask your paediatrician or a lactation consultant to check this.

Nipple infection

Cracked nipples can sometimes become infected with:
- bacteria (*Staphylococcus aureus* or 'Staph')
- thrush *(Candida albicans)*
- or both.

It can be difficult to diagnose which of these is causing problems. Sometimes, nipple thrush *may* follow a course of antibiotics.

Symptoms of nipple infection may include sore nipples and shooting pains in the breast. Not only is nipple infection particularly painful, but it can be passed back and forth between mother and baby.

Research has not come up with one standard treatment for nipple infection. Different doctors treat it differently, depending on their own clinical experience. If the doctor suspects thrush, treatment is likely to involve an oral gel or drops for baby's mouth, an ointment for the mother's nipples and sometimes another one for baby's bottom. Antifungal tablets may also be prescribed for the mother. If Staph is suspected, antibiotic ointment and/or possibly oral antibiotics may be prescribed for the mother. Some doctors may prescribe a combination treatment for the nipples.

Extra first aid for cracked nipples
The first aid measures for sore nipples work for cracked nipples as well.

The following strategies may also help:

- Pay special attention to getting your baby well attached.
- Start each feed on the good side and make sure you drain the breast well.
- Bacteria can enter through the crack and an infection may follow. Be especially careful to keep anything that comes in contact with the nipple as clean as possible. Smear some breastmilk onto your nipple after feeding or expressing. After each feed, check whether the crack has become worse.
- As a last resort, you may have to take your baby off your sore breast temporarily, to rest the nipple until it begins to heal.
- If this happens, you will need to express your milk by hand or with a good-quality breast pump on a gentle setting. You can feed your expressed milk to your baby by cup, spoon or syringe. As soon as the crack has improved, gradually reintroduce the breast. Make sure your baby is not too hungry and keep the first feeds short. Take special care to get your baby's attachment as perfect as possible. Continue to express from that breast and use the milk to top up your baby until you are back to full feeding.
- If neither feeding at the breast nor expressing is working, you might need to try a soft nipple shield. There is a variety of these available. Some are likely to fit your unique size and shape better than others. Some mothers find that the friction of a shield on the nipple while the baby is feeding makes the pain worse. On the other hand, some mothers find them very helpful and have used them successfully for varying lengths of time. When using a nipple shield, it is important to learn how to use it properly. This usually involves a face-to-face consultation with a health professional (such as a lactation consultant) or a breastfeeding counsellor.

Blocked duct

Sometimes a duct (which carries milk from the glands in the breast) becomes squashed, narrowed or completely blocked. If you have a lumpy or engorged area on your breast, which feels sore or looks red, you probably have a blocked duct. If you

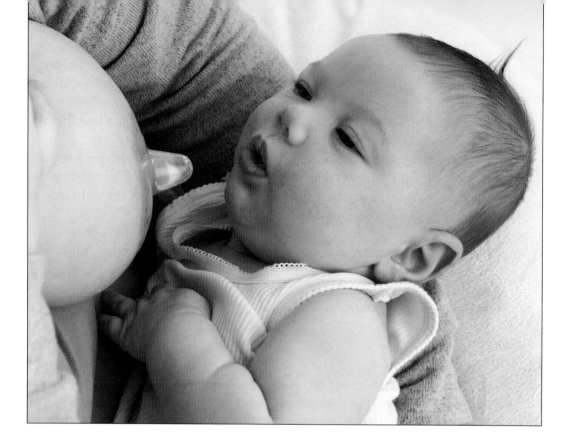

have had breast surgery in the past, you will need to be especially careful to check for blockages while breastfeeding.

Milk ducts, on average, are only 2 mm in diameter, so it's easy to see how blockages can occur from time to time. Milk then banks up behind the blockage, a lump forms and your breast begins to feel sore.

Clearing blocked ducts:

- **Start treatment immediately**. Otherwise your breast may become inflamed and you may begin to feel feverish. See your doctor if this happens or if you can't clear the blocked duct within 12 hours.
- **Feed from the affected breast first.** Your baby's suck will be stronger at the start of each feed and the suction will help get rid of the blockage.
- **Feed more frequently than usual.** Start each feed from the affected breast and let your baby feed as long as possible on this side. Make sure the other breast doesn't become over full. Express if necessary to avoid this.
- **Apply warmth before a feed.** Heat is comforting and helps clear a blockage by encouraging the let-down reflex. Have a warm shower or soak your breasts in

comfortably warm water in the bath or in a bowl. You can also use a well covered hot water bottle, a warm towel or face washer wrung out in very warm water, or a commercial heat pack. Take care not to burn yourself.

- **Massage the affected area.** Gently but firmly massage the lump towards the nipple during and after feeds.
- **Change feeding positions to help drain the breast.** If you choose positions that allow the milk to flow 'downhill' to your baby, gravity helps the flow. So feeding while lying on your left side might help a blockage on the right side of either nipple. You can even try feeding on all fours.
- **Hand express** if necessary to drain your breasts.
- **Make your breasts more comfortable.** Loosen your bra, or better still, take it off during feeds (or even between feeds if it helps).
- **Use cold packs** after a feed to relieve pain and reduce inflammation.
- **Rest as much as possible.**

Mastitis

Mastitis literally means an inflammation of the breast. Many people believe that any mastitis is a breast infection. However redness, pain and heat in the breast don't necessarily mean that there is a bacterial infection present.

Most cases of mastitis occur when a milk duct in the breast becomes blocked. If you only have these symptoms, you may be able to treat the problem yourself:

- Feed your baby more frequently than usual.
- Apply warmth to the tender area just before feeding your baby, and cold packs afterwards and between feeds.
- Give yourself a break from your regular activities, stay home and rest.
- However, if you cannot clear the lump in 12 hours or if you develop a high temperature, chills, aches and other flu-like symptoms, you will need to see your medical adviser.

What causes mastitis?
A number of factors increase your chances of developing mastitis, including:

- an ongoing blockage in a milk duct or nipple opening
- poor attachment
- regularly missing feeds, infrequent feeds, scheduling feeds or restricting the length of feeds
- cracked or grazed nipples (usually resulting from poor attachment)

- an oversupply of milk
- rapid weaning
- pressure on the breast, most commonly from a poorly-fitting bra, tight clothing or, for some, simply wearing a bra to bed. Car seatbelts or sleeping on your tummy may also cause problems.
- using pressure on the breast to restrict milk flow during a feed
- any injury to a breast or previous breast surgery
- if you are sick, very tired or stressed.

Prevention is better than cure

As with most breastfeeding problems, prevention is better than cure. It will help if you watch for any telltale signs, while following some simple tips.

- Make sure your baby is well positioned at every feed so that she drains each breast effectively.
- Don't restrict either the number or length of feeds.
- Express after a feed if your baby hasn't fed well and your breasts still feel very full.
- Check your breasts each day for signs of lumps, redness or nipple damage.
- If they become tender, apply some warmth to the breast before feeds and gently massage away any lumpy areas while you are feeding. Use cold compresses after the feed to reduce inflammation.
- Get as much rest as you can, particularly in the first 3 months.
- Don't smoke — it lowers your resistance to infection.

Treating mastitis

If you're unlucky enough to have mastitis, the first rule is: ***Keep breastfeeding!*** Effective removal of breastmilk is the most important step towards recovering from a bout of mastitis.

Some women are told not to breastfeed during a bout of mastitis. This advice is wrong. There is no evidence that your milk poses a health risk to your baby. Your breastmilk has antibacterial properties that protect your baby. You will also be in severe pain if you stop breastfeeding.

- **Feed frequently.** Letting the milk bank up in the breast will make the condition much worse. Begin each feed on the affected breast. If the pain in the sore breast is so severe that your let-down is affected, start with the other breast and swap sides as soon as your milk begins to flow.

- **Vary the feeding position.** This helps to drain all the areas of the breast.
- **Massage.** Gently massage the breast towards the nipple during the feed and finish each feed by expressing. This helps the breast to drain and speeds up your recovery.
- **Warmth.** Applying warmth to the sore breast before you feed can be very comforting.
- **Rest.** If possible, rest in bed with your baby close to you so you don't have to get up and down. Have everything you might need at hand including water and a nutritious snack.
- **Medication.** If you have tried all these strategies over the past 24 hours and things are not improving, or if it's only been a few hours and you are feeling extremely unwell, you should make an urgent appointment with your doctor as you may need antibiotics. Your doctor will be able to prescribe a medication that is safe when breastfeeding and may also suggest a painkiller to help with the aches and pains. Even if the mastitis is non-infective (and it is impossible for your doctor to be able to tell whether it is or not) antibiotics have an anti-inflammatory action, which will help reduce your symptoms. If an antibiotic is prescribed, be sure to finish the whole course to avoid a recurrence of the problem.

Breast abscess

A breast abscess is a localised collection of pus that forms when a bacterial infection hasn't drained. It is usually a complication of infective mastitis that has been poorly treated. It is most likely to occur when a mother weans during a bout of breast inflammation. Symptoms of a breast abscess include nausea, extreme fatigue and aching muscles, in addition to swelling, pain and redness in the affected area. A breast abscess requires surgical drainage as well as antibiotic therapy and rest. While you are treated by your doctors (you will probably need to see a specialist) it's important that you keep the breast well drained.

You can usually continue to feed your baby while you are being treated and return to full breastfeeding after it has healed.

CHAPTER 15

Tummy troubles

Wind

Colic

What causes colic?

Soothing and comforting your
colicky baby

Gastro-oesophageal reflux

Lactose intolerance

Allergies

Some babies suffer with tummy problems more than others. Seeing your baby in pain is very stressful. The term 'colic' is often used to describe what appears to be tummy pain, but should not be confused with 'wind'. While wind can cause a baby brief discomfort (and sometimes some pain), colic can cause frequent bouts of intense pain that occurs often. Sometimes gastro-oesophageal reflux is also confused with colic, as they both cause great distress in babies.

Wind

Wind generally refers to the bubble of air brought up during or soon after a feed. Most new mothers think their baby has to burp at the end of every feed. Some babies will respond with an adult-size burp. Others never seem to bring up much wind. A baby can easily swallow and breathe while feeding unless the flow of milk is too fast. Everyone swallows air when they eat and it is not usually a problem. However, some babies seem to take in more air during feeding than others. They may make strange faces and seem unhappy. This doesn't necessarily mean your baby is in pain or has colic.

There are some simple ways to help your baby bring up wind:
- **Hold him upright** to help the bubble of wind rise from his stomach.
- **Hold him with his tummy against your shoulder.** Gently rub or pat his back.
- **Sit your baby on your lap,** supporting his chin with one hand, and put your other hand on his back. Again, gently rub or pat his back.
- **Lay your baby on his back**, his body flat on your lap for about a minute, then raise him gently to sitting position, keeping his back straight.
- **Drape him across the top of one of your legs** (so that your thigh is the main point of contact with his tummy). Support his head with one hand and gently rub his back with the other.
- **Lay your baby on his tummy along your forearm,** with his head near the crook of your elbow and your hand holding his nappy area.

Colic

Colic affects even healthy babies. It usually starts around 2 weeks and ends around 3 months of age. There is usually no clear pattern to the crying except that it is likely to be at its worst during the early evening hours. A baby is defined as having colic if he cries at least 3 hours a day, for 3 days a week over a period of at least 3 weeks.

If your baby has colic:

- He may first begin to squirm and fuss, sucking at his hands and showing all the signs of hunger. However, when you put him to the breast, he will feed eagerly for a few minutes, then stop and cry or scream.
- He may settle for a short while, only to wake again crying.
- During colic attacks, his face will go red and he will frown. His pupils may dilate as if he is frightened.
- He may draw his legs up to his tummy, with sharp, shrill cries.
- Picking him up doesn't seem to comfort him.
- He stops crying only when the spasm ends. Each attack may last 4–5 minutes. He may drift off to sleep but another attack soon wakes him. This may be repeated many times and everyone ends up exhausted and upset.
- Sometimes he also has loud tummy gurgles, burps a lot or passes wind from the bowel. This may give him some relief, as does passing a bowel motion or sucking. The baby's desire to suck often makes a mother think her baby is hungry when it is actually colic.

What causes colic?

No-one really knows what causes colic. It is likely that there is more than one cause. One theory supported by research suggests that the baby who is switched to the second breast too early may take too much milk, too quickly. Switching breasts gives the baby another large volume of low-fat milk from the second breast, rather than the smaller volume of creamier milk he would get if he stayed on the first breast. This means he takes in more lactose than he can easily break down and absorb. The excess lactose moves from the small bowel into the large bowel. The bacteria in the large bowel ferment the lactose. This process produces gas that causes colic, wind and frequent loose and sometimes explosive bowel actions. More fat in the breastmilk slows down the rate at which the stomach empties and the overall speed of the food travelling through his system. This allows more time for the baby to digest the lactose. A baby who takes large, low-fat feeds may still act like he is hungry, wanting to suck frequently for comfort. However, this simply makes the problem worse.

Other research shows that a small number of babies seem to react to certain foods in their mothers' diets. Some babies react to caffeine, which is found in tea, coffee, chocolate and cola drinks. When these mothers cut out caffeine, their babies no longer cried as much. Other babies react to cows' milk, wheat or soy. If you think your baby is reacting to something in your diet, you should seek professional advice before making major changes to what you eat. Any big change in your diet (eg giving up dairy products) should only be done under the care of a dietitian or allergy specialist. You need to be sure you are still getting a balanced diet.

Yet another theory is that colic can be caused by a sensory overload. These babies need quiet surroundings and soothing, calm handling until their colic resolves.

Soothing and comforting your colicky baby

Infant formula is not as easily digested as breastmilk and formula-fed babies also suffer with colic. Breastmilk is still the best food for your baby and most colicky babies seem to grow well. As your baby grows, his digestive system will mature.

In the meantime, there are a number of things that might comfort your baby:

- **Make feed times as gentle and relaxing as possible.** Feed him before he reaches the point of crying to be fed.
- **Carry him around as much as you can,** as this is a simple way to rock him. Crying, colicky babies are seldom seen in countries where babies are carried around until they can walk. A baby sling will allow you to carry your baby upright and leave your hands free.

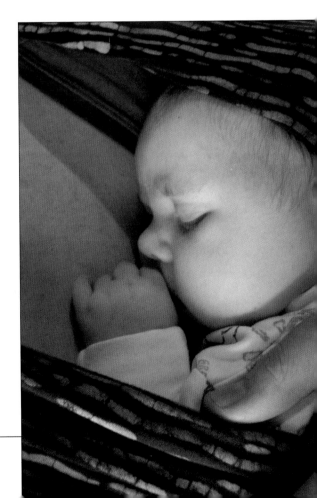

- **Wrap him snugly** in a warm, soft material, such as cotton or light wool.
- **Colicky babies prefer being upright** and/or having pressure on their tummies.
- Some colicky babies cry in their sleep without waking. **Wait to see if he drifts back to sleep before you pick him up,** but don't let him get distressed. Have him sleep near you so you can watch and assess whether he needs you to comfort him or leave him alone.

- **A dummy can help if your older baby gets comfort from sucking,** but his constant suckling is giving you too much milk. It will not work if your baby is hungry, so only offer the dummy if you are sure he has had a good feed. Sucking is good for colicky babies as it helps expel the gas by moving it through the bowel.
- **If you have too much milk** (as shown by more than 10 wet nappies and many bowel motions a day), feed your baby on only one side per feed. If he wants to suck often, try 'block feeding'. This means you offer the same side for two or more feeds in a row, over a period of 3–4 or more hours. Watch out for blocked ducts in the 'unused' breast. You may only need to do this for a few days before returning to a more normal feeding pattern. See Chapter 13 for more hints.
- **If your let-down reflex is very strong,** your baby may have trouble coping with the flow. It can help if you express some milk before a feed and wait until the first rush of milk has slowed before offering him the breast.
- Lying down to feed is one way of **slowing the flow.** Another way is to recline, so that your baby is sucking 'uphill'. You can do this by attaching him while sitting, then lying back with your baby on your tummy. Or you can begin in a reclining position and let your baby self-attach.

General tips for soothing your baby:
- **Let your baby kick on the floor** for a while, or you can move his legs with a gentle bicycle action.
- **Baby massage** can relax and comfort babies, especially those with colic.
- **Keep the room warm**, but avoid overheating.
- **A warm bath or shower** with a parent often helps babies relax.
- **A walk outside** or around the block can relax you both.
- Try **gently rolling the pram** back and forth as you sit or stand. It sometimes helps to roll over a slight bump (such as a folded towel) or where there is a change in floor coverings.
- Rhythmic, **continuous 'white noise'**, such as a washing machine or vacuum cleaner can help lull your baby to sleep.
- **Playing music** with a soft melody or a definite beat, or singing to your baby can be soothing.

While most colicky babies thrive and the colic passes, living with a baby who cries a lot is very stressful. If it lasts even for 3 months, it can seem like a lifetime. See your medical adviser regularly to make sure that he is growing well. Call in all your favours and ask family and friends to lend a hand with housework, shopping and cooking. Meanwhile, focus on soothing your baby and getting as much support as possible.

Gastro-oesophageal reflux

Gastro-oesophageal reflux happens when the contents of the stomach come back up into the oesophagus (the tube that connects the mouth to the stomach). There are two levels of this condition — gastro-oesophageal reflux (simple reflux) and gastro-oesophageal reflux disease (GORD).

Simple reflux
Two out of three healthy babies bring up milk at least once a day; many do so several times a day. However, they are generally happy and content and putting on weight. This is simple reflux. It doesn't hurt the baby and it stops by itself as the baby grows. It can be hard to tell whether a baby is simply bringing up extra milk or vomiting. Vomiting is when there is more force and larger amounts of milk.

Reflux is more likely to happen when your baby is lying down, when his stomach is very full or when there is pressure on his tummy (maybe from a tight nappy, clothing or a seat belt). It can also be worse when he's slumped or curled (maybe in a baby capsule or sling) or when he's having a nappy change or bath.

> Not all babies with reflux actually bring up milk. Instead of coming all the way up and out of the baby's mouth, it goes back into the stomach. This is called 'silent reflux'.

Reflux commonly starts to improve after 6–7 months. It is usually gone by about 12–18 months of age. This is because your baby stays more upright as he begins to sit, stand and then walk. Also, the oesophagus gets longer as he grows. If he still has symptoms by 24 months, it may mean a more long-term problem. Your medical adviser will need to assess this.

Some practical suggestions
The ideas for babies with colic can also work well for babies with simple reflux. You could also try some of the following:
- **Calm your baby before feeding.** An upset baby is more likely to vomit.
- After a feed, while his stomach is at its fullest, **lay him on his left side**. In this position, the point where his oesophagus joins the stomach is higher.
- **Keep him more upright** during nappy changes by raising the head end of your change table or propping him up on a pillow or foam wedge on a change mat. Instead of raising his legs to clean his bottom, roll him over to one side.
- Adjust the pram so that **he isn't lying flat.**

- **Avoid pressure on the stomach** from tight nappies or pants.
- Short periods in a reclining baby chair may help but **don't allow him to slump over,** as this puts more pressure on his tummy.
- Use gentle handling, as babies with reflux don't cope well with being jiggled or passed from person to person.
- **Playtime is better before a feed** when his tummy is emptier.
- If he vomits often, the skin around his mouth may get red and sore. **Use a soft cloth to wipe his face** instead of a baby wipe or tissue. A soothing barrier cream (like the highly purified lanolin often sold for sore nipples) can help. Try using only pure soap to wash his clothing and bedding.

Reflux can mean lots of cleaning up and washing. Your baby will often be distressed and wake frequently at night. You may need to carry him upright to help him keep his feeds down. You may also worry about his health and weight gains. This will all take its toll on both you and your partner. In some parts of Australia, there are special support groups for parents living with a baby with reflux. The support of others who are going through the same thing can be reassuring. A good place to look is: *reflux.org.au*

Gastro-oesophageal reflux disease (GORD)

GORD is a medical condition and needs to be managed by your baby's doctor. The symptoms are:

- bringing up a large amount of milk after most feeds, especially if it is coloured
- sleep problems. He's easily woken, especially by noise. He may settle after a feed but wake when he is laid flat in his cot.
- coughing, wheezing or constant snuffles
- frequent ear infections
- lots of dribbling
- crying and irritability
- bowel motions that contain mucus or look slimy
- feeding problems — very frequent feeding or breast refusal (sometimes both)
- burping, gurgling noises, hiccups or even trouble burping.

There can be other causes of these symptoms too. They do not always mean GORD. For example, reflux and the symptoms listed above can also be caused by food allergy or food intolerance in a baby. A skilled medical diagnosis is needed so that your baby can receive proper care. This will often involve the simple reflux techniques as well as medication. It may also involve dietary investigation.

Breastmilk will continue to play an important role in the care of a baby with GORD.

Lactose intolerance

It is common for breastfed babies to have many loose bowel motions. This does not mean they have lactose intolerance. A baby who is switched from one breast to the other without the chance to drain the first breast may sometimes show symptoms similar to lactose intolerance.

Allowing the baby to drain the breast usually overcomes this. 'Block feeding' may help in many cases (see page 138). A mother with an oversupply of breastmilk may also see these symptoms in her baby.

Primary (or true) lactose intolerance is a very rare condition where the lactose in milk — the main carbohydrate in all mammals' milk — cannot be digested by the baby. The symptoms begin at birth and are watery, acidic diarrhoea, wind in the bowel, a bloated abdomen and failure to thrive.

Secondary lactose intolerance is more common. It is a result of subtle damage to the lining of the digestive system. This may be caused by a bout of gastroenteritis (especially a rotavirus infection), or an allergy or intolerance to a food protein from the mother's diet passing into her milk. The enzyme lactase is needed to digest lactose. It is produced in the very tips of folds in the intestine. Anything that causes damage to the intestine may wipe off these tips and reduce the amount of the enzyme.

Secondary lactose intolerance is temporary, as long as the cause of the gut damage is removed, giving it a chance to heal. For example, if the food to which a breastfed baby is allergic is taken out of the mother's diet, the intestine will heal, even if the baby is still having breastmilk. If your doctor does diagnose 'lactose intolerance', continuing to breastfeed will not harm your baby as long as he is growing normally.

While a baby shows symptoms of lactose intolerance, it is sometimes suggested that the mother alternate breastfeeding the baby with feeds of lactose-free formula. She may even be told to take the baby off the breast. However, medical authorities recommend the use of lactose-free formula only if the baby is formula-fed and is very malnourished and/or losing weight.

Human milk remains the best food and will assist with gut healing. In addition, allergy or intolerance of the baby to foreign protein (cow or soy) should be considered before starting any formula.

This includes lactose-free milk that is made from cows' milk, as this may make the problem worse. You should seek professional advice on the need for hypoallergenic formula that is available on prescription. The partially hydrolysed hypo-allergenic formulas (called 'HA') are unsuitable for a baby already showing symptoms. A paediatric specialist should see any baby who has long-term symptoms and/or is failing to thrive.

For more information, read the article on the ABA website, *Lactose intolerance and the breastfed baby,* by Joy Anderson BSc(Nutrition), PostgradDipDiet, APD, IBCLC, ABA Breastfeeding Counsellor .

Allergies

If you or your partner have allergies, you may be concerned that you will pass the condition on. This can happen in a small number of breastfed babies. If your baby is reacting to foods through your milk, then you will need to avoid them while breastfeeding. Giving infant formula feeds soon after birth might trigger cows' milk allergy in a baby prone to allergy, even if he is later fully breastfed.

In the early months, when your baby's digestive system is not yet mature, whole foreign proteins transfer from breastmilk into the bloodstream more easily than when he is older.

Babies can be unsettled because they are reacting to something the mother ate. However, it is less common than most people think. Weaning usually makes the baby's condition worse.

Contrary to popular belief, soy-based or goats'-milk infant formulas do not protect against allergies. Protein in each of these is as foreign as cows'-milk protein and can also cause an antibody response. You should always seek expert help from an accredited practising dietitian specialising in food allergy and intolerance before you make any big changes to your normal diet. If you need to prepare special food for yourself and your baby, this can mean extra work and cost. You also need to check that you are getting all the nutrients both you and your baby need. Ask your doctor for a referral to a specialist who can give you skilled advice.

CHAPTER 16

Food fights

Breast refusal

Biting and teething

What if your baby isn't
breastfeeding well?

What if your baby completely
refuses to breastfeed?

Sucking difficulties

Tongue-tie

All the books tell you that babies love breastfeeding and that they instinctively 'root' for the breast and seek the nipple. What if your baby refuses to suck and, in fact, seems to fight the breast every time you offer it? Or what if she just can't seem to suck properly?

Breast refusal

Breast refusal can happen out of the blue or gradually creep up on you. Reasons vary with your baby's stage of development. Her refusal can take a number of forms:
- She may suck for a few minutes, then break away with signs of distress and may refuse to continue.
- She may refuse even to begin sucking, although she is obviously hungry.
- Sometimes, your baby may not actually refuse to feed, but will be very fussy and difficult to feed. She may seem unwilling to start sucking or take a long time to get going. When she stops feeding, she may still seem restless and fidgety.

It is very upsetting if your baby refuses to feed properly. Your main concern is that your baby will starve if you can't get her to take milk over several hours. Added to this, when your baby turns away from your breast, it may feel as though she is rejecting you as a mother. In this situation, you may believe that you have no choice but to stop breastfeeding. Fortunately, this needn't be the case. Breast refusal is usually a temporary problem and there are strategies you can use to get past it.

Some reasons for refusal in the early weeks:
- Sometimes a baby refuses to feed **because she is tired**, particularly straight after the birth if you have been given drugs during labour. She may just like to nuzzle and lick. Forcing her to the breast before she is ready will upset her (and you). Encourage her by expressing a little colostrum into her mouth. If she still refuses, don't worry, just tuck her in skin-to-skin with you and give her a little more time. She may show more interest when she is more alert.
- **Touching or pushing the back of her head** as you try to get her attached can make her refuse. Even clothing around her neck and chin can interfere with her natural 'rooting' reflex. When you touch her cheek, your newborn baby will automatically turn and lift her head towards that side. Holding her head or touching both cheeks will confuse her and may cause her to fuss, shake her head or appear to refuse the breast. A baby who is uncomfortable will not feed well.
- After the milk comes in, your breasts are very full. Express a little milk before you feed so that the **areola is soft enough for your baby to latch on to.**
- Your baby may find it **hard to coordinate sucking, swallowing and breathing.**

If her nose is covered by her top lip or the breast, it will make it harder for her to breathe. Nor is she likely to be attached to the breast properly. If your breast is very full, lift it up slightly with your free hand. Holding your baby on her side and wrapping her body closer in around your tummy should help bring her nose away from the breast and her chin towards it. This is much more effective than pressing on your breast with your finger to create an air passage.

- **If your newborn baby has received bottles,** she may already be used to the different sucking action required by a bottle teat. She may take a little time to adjust. It will be quicker and easier if she has no more bottles.
- **A sudden gushing flow of milk** can make your baby gag and frighten her. Express a little before the feed until the flow settles down. If she pulls away during a feed because of fast flow, wait till the flow slows before starting again.

Some reasons for later refusal:
- A baby who has **struggled to cope with a very fast flow** in the early months and has never seemed to enjoy feeds may begin to refuse at about 3–4 months when she has more control of her own movements.
- If your baby has been **used to milk just pouring into her mouth,** she may not have learned to milk the breast efficiently, so when your supply settles down and she needs to actually milk the breast, she may initially be fussy and irritable.
- She may be frustrated if **her appetite cannot be satisfied** with the milk available and shows this frustration by refusing to feed.
- If your **let-down reflex takes longer than before** to get going, your baby may become impatient. Try to trigger the let-down reflex before a feed.
- Your baby may also fight the breast if she is **overtired or over-stimulated.** Try to make her day as low-key as possible until the problem resolves.
- **A blocked nose** may make it difficult to breathe and feed, so she may refuse.
- **A baby with gastric reflux** may be fussy when laid down flat to feed. Ask your medical adviser to check your baby.
- **Teething discomfort** can also cause your baby to refuse to feed and may occur weeks before a tooth appears.
- Between the ages of 4–6 months, babies are very **easily distracted.** Feeding in a quiet room may help.
- When your baby **starts on other foods or drinks**, she may refuse the breast if she has had bottles or cups of infant formula, boiled water or fruit juice. Her appetite for your milk will be less and your supply may drop. Your baby may also have become used to the different sucking action of the bottle. Unless you are actively trying to wean, give extra breastfeeds rather than bottle-feeds.

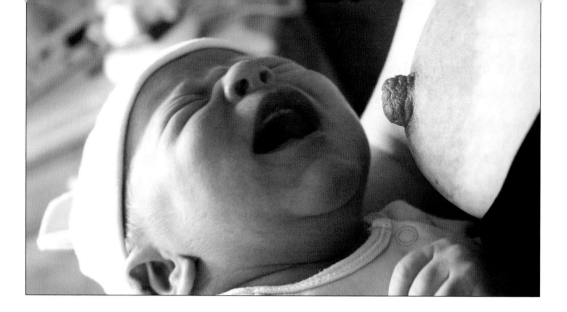

Refusing just one breast:

- If your newborn consistently has problems feeding from a particular breast, or lying on one side, you might like to have her checked by a health professional. Sometimes babies are stiff on one side from their **position in the womb, or from events during the birth.**
- If your baby has fallen asleep after one breast, she may **simply have had enough.** Not all babies feed from both breasts every feed.
- Many babies **favour one breast** because the milk may flow more freely from that breast, but occasionally because they just have a preference for lying on that side. If she has a sore leg or arm after immunisation, she may suddenly refuse to feed on one side because she is lying on a sore spot.
- If she has **an ear infection,** she may also refuse the breast, as lying down makes the pain worse.

'Am I the problem?' There are a number of possible mother-centred factors:

- **A sudden change in your diet** can affect the taste of your milk and the smell of your body, causing your baby to refuse to feed.
- **A new perfume** or spray deodorant, strong detergents that affect the smell of your bra, chlorine from a pool, even smells from the hairdresser, may possibly cause your baby to refuse. A quick shower will usually solve this problem.
- **Are you menstruating or ovulating?** Hormonal changes can temporarily affect the taste of your milk. For some women, their baby fussing at the breast is an early warning that their period is due.
- **Pregnancy** can also cause a drop in the milk supply or a change in the taste.

- **Some hormonal contraceptives** have an effect on the taste of breastmilk. Make sure your doctor is aware that you are breastfeeding before a hormonal contraceptive is prescribed. Even some contraceptives which are routinely used for breastfeeding women can affect some babies. If you feel that this might be the problem, you may need to offer more frequent feeds until your baby gets used to the change in taste. Or use another method of contraception for a while.

Changing needs

The amount of time your baby takes to get the milk she needs can change from feed to feed, from week to week. If you're used to her taking 20 minutes each breast, you might be concerned if she just takes 5 minutes or only wants one side. This isn't necessarily a case of breast refusal, but more likely she's got all she needs quite quickly.

Sometimes, your baby is just not hungry as often as she was in the past. Feeding patterns do change. A previously enthusiastic feeder may start to be more interested in her surroundings than your breast. Most babies have longer breaks between feeds as they grow older. If there is no apparent reason for your baby refusing to breastfeed — and you have tried the suggestions to help and your baby is well — it might mean that she is heading towards weaning herself. This may come as a shock if you had planned to wean her slowly much later.

If your baby weans suddenly you will need to express occasionally to ensure that your breasts do not become overfull and uncomfortable.

Tips to deal with breast refusal:
- **Don't force her head onto the breast.** If she is refusing and struggling at the breast, take a break and try again a little later when you are both calm.
- **Offer the breast as soon as your baby begins to wake,** or even while she is still half asleep. She will usually respond better if she is not upset or crying. Change her nappy after the feed or before the second breast.
- **Check that your baby is comfortable and correctly positioned.** Try baby-led attachment as described in Chapter 5.
- **Make sure you are comfortable and relaxed.**
- **Gently help your baby take the breast into her mouth.** If you have large nipples, try to shape the breast between your thumb and fingers so that it is easier for her to grasp. If your nipples are very small, try to pull them out gently just before you offer the breast.
- **Express your milk until it begins to flow** easily so that your baby will get milk as soon as she starts to suck.

- **Offer her a little expressed breastmilk** via a cup or spoon before a breastfeed to take the edge off her appetite and calm her.
- **Spend time skin-to-skin,** carrying or cuddling your baby without offering the breast, so she can enjoy the closeness and breastfeed when she is ready to.
- **Take a warm bath together**. Many babies then relax and feed well.

Biting and teething

When a baby is breastfeeding correctly, she is not able to bite, because her tongue is over her bottom gum (and teeth). It is when babies are not actively feeding that they are more likely to bite. This is usually at the beginning of the feed or at the end when you are not paying full attention to her.

A teething baby whose gums are tender often likes to bite and chew and might do so while attempting to feed. Giving her something hard and cold to chew on or rubbing her gums before a feed may relieve her discomfort. This may make her less likely to chew on the breast. If you feel your baby is in pain, you may need to consult your pharmacist or doctor for pain relief or a teething gel.

Some babies with newly-erupted teeth will 'rest' these teeth on the mother's areola or breast, leaving little indentations that, although not a bite, can be quite painful. At times like this it helps to go back to basics with positioning and attachment. Take care when you are feeding that your baby is held closely chest-to-chest, has a big wide mouth and has her chin to your breast. Careful positioning and attachment, and a little time for those very sharp top teeth to smooth down, and you will soon be feeding in comfort again.

Some mothers find that changes in the teething baby's saliva can irritate the nipples. Rinsing the nipple area after feeds with a little bicarbonate of soda dissolved in water (approximately 1 teaspoon to 1 cup), bathing in salty water or even a swim in the ocean, may relieve soreness of this kind.

A nipple that has been bitten by baby's sharp new teeth can be treated in the same way as a sore or cracked nipple — a smear of breastmilk after a feed, exposure to fresh air, and prompt changing of damp nursing pads or bras. See your medical adviser if these measures do not promote healing, or if the area becomes inflamed or infected.

Watch your baby while she feeds and if she just seems to be playing or gets a mischievous look in her eye, break the suction and stop breastfeeding. If she does bite, say 'No!' as calmly as you can and take her off the breast straight away. She will soon get the message.

Try to avoid a loud 'Ouch!' as this may either frighten your baby or, alternatively, amuse her, so she may try it again. Sometimes, a baby who has been frightened by her mother's reaction to being bitten refuses to go back to the breast. Try the suggestions to get baby back to the breast. Biting, if it does occur, is usually just a temporary (and painful) stage. A nip can hurt even when your baby has no teeth but it is usually associated with teething. Most babies never bite but even those who do have a biting phase often continue to breastfeed throughout toddlerhood without further problems.

What if your baby isn't breastfeeding well?

- **Some sleepy babies may need to be woken for feeds** so that they gain enough weight. Most breastfed babies need to feed at least 8–12 times in 24 hours. This is approximately every 2–3 hours, day and night, during the first weeks of life. If you are worried about your baby's weight gain, you may need to wake and feed her more often, including at least once during the night. It may also be possible to feed a baby without waking her.
- You may find it helps to **change sides several times during a feed,** whenever your baby's sucking slows. This often makes her suck more strongly and triggers a good let-down reflex. If your baby stays on one breast, she may just doze for much of the time. Swapping sides will drain both breasts better and help more milk to be made. After feeding from each breast the first time, your baby will get creamier milk when feeding from them a second or third time.
- It may help to stroke all around your breast from your chest wall towards the nipple as your baby feeds. Another way of helping the milk flow to your baby is to use **'breast compression'.** Gently squeeze a large handful of your breast as your baby feeds. Hold for as long as she is drinking well. When she slows, move your hand to a different part of your breast and squeeze again. Take care not to disturb the nipple in your baby's mouth.
- Lots of **cuddling skin-to-skin** with your baby helps your hormones to act. In fact, skin-to-skin contact has been found to increase the volume of breastmilk a mother can express by up to one and a half times.

What if your baby completely refuses to breastfeed?

It is very important to protect your milk supply by pumping by hand or a good quality manual or electric breast pump. It is easier to express once you have had a let-down.

You can feed expressed breastmilk to your baby with a small cup, spoon or syringe. Even newborn babies can drink very well from a cup.

If she is having trouble learning how to attach to the breast, a bottle may confuse her and make it even harder for her to learn how to breastfeed.

Sucking difficulties

Sucking problems can result in slow weight gains and failure to thrive in a baby, as well as nipple problems, mastitis and low milk supply in a mother.

A small number of babies need help to learn to suck effectively. This is more common in premature babies, those born before 34 weeks gestation when the suck-swallow instinct is not well developed, or in babies who are ill. Occasionally, babies have sucking problems because of poor reflexes, or because they have poor mouth closure, or have suffered some sort of birth trauma.

Most cases of poor sucking are caused by interference in the natural process of birth and establishment of breastfeeding (giving bottle-feeds or dummies), separating mother and baby at birth (so breastfeeding establishment is delayed), drugs given in labour that interfere with the baby's ability to suck, or the wrong use of nipple shields.

In some situations, a baby can benefit from special 'suck training'. This training should be provided by a lactation consultant, speech pathologist or occupational therapist with relevant skills and experience. They will teach you techniques so that the three of you can work together as a team to overcome the problem.

Tongue-tie

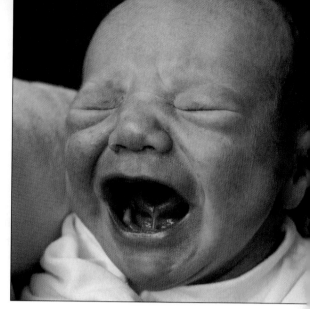

Another cause of poor sucking is 'tongue-tie', where the tongue is anchored too tightly to the floor of the mouth so that it is not mobile enough for the baby to attach properly to the breast. Tongue-tie occurs in about 5% of people, is three times more common in males and runs in families. It can cause difficulty with breastfeeding and may lead to dental or speech problems later in life if not treated.

Babies need good tongue movement to be able to attach to and remove milk optimally from the breast. Hence, babies with a tongue-tie often have poor tongue movement so they often are unable to remove milk optimally from the breast. They also often have difficulty opening wide enough to take in a full mouthful of breast tissue. This can result in 'nipple-feeding' because the nipple is not drawn far enough back towards the junction of the hard and soft palates. The mother is more likely to suffer nipple trauma as her nipple is constantly beating against the baby's hard palate during feeding.

Early release (or snipping) of a diagnosed tongue-tie can help prevent the baby from forming a habit of movements to compensate for the tongue-tie that may be difficult to deal with at a later stage. You will be helped to breastfeed immediately after the procedure to encourage optimal movement of the tongue and to distract the baby from any discomfort.

Breastfeeding was uncomfortable and not quite what I expected. My baby was taking over an hour to feed and I was sore. After leaving hospital it went from bad to worse, with my nipples eventually cracking and bleeding.

Then a child and family health service midwife told me that my baby was tongue-tied and booked her in the next day to fix it. The very next feed after her 'snip' was like heaven. It confirmed that I was doing it right.

The let-down reflex

Keeping things clean

How to hand express

Breast pumps

How much to express

Containers for storing breastmilk

Cleaning containers and breast
pump parts

Handling breastmilk

Feeding EBM to your baby

The best way to remove milk from your breasts is by breastfeeding. However, there may be times when this is not possible and you need to express so that your baby is still able to receive your breastmilk.

There might be situations where:
- Your breasts feel too full or uncomfortable or your nipples are very sore.
- You need to go out and leave your baby with a sitter or carer.
- You are going back to paid work, study or other commitments.
- Your baby is refusing to breastfeed.
- Your baby can't suck because he was premature, or has a cleft lip/palate or other problems with sucking.
- Your baby is in hospital and you can't be there for every feed.
- You need to be in hospital and your baby can't be with you for every feed.
- You are using a breast pump to relactate or induce lactation.
- You want to keep a small store of breastmilk in the freezer for emergencies, to avoid having to give your baby formula.

The let-down reflex

Being able to remove milk from the breast depends on the let-down reflex. This reflex happens in response to your baby's sucking. The sight or sound of your baby, or even just thinking of him, can make it happen.

The let-down reflex happens more than once during a feed or expressing session. However, most mothers will only notice the first. Swapping breasts when the flow slows helps trigger more let-downs while you're expressing.

Ways you can help your milk to let down when you are expressing:
- **Relax**. If possible, express in a quiet, pleasant area, where there is nothing to distract you. This could be where you usually sit to feed. While you express, breathe slowly and deeply. Some mothers have a warm drink first or listen to soft music. Warmth may also help. Express after a warm shower, or place warm face washers on the breast for a few minutes before starting.
- **Gently massage your breasts.** Stroke your breast towards the nipple with the flat of your hand or edge of a finger. Gently roll the nipples between your fingers. While this will not actually push the milk out of your breasts, it can help trigger the let-down reflex.
- **Think about your baby.** If you are expressing because he is premature or sick

in hospital, you might find it easier to express while you are there close to him, or just after you leave him. While you are away from him you might find just looking at his photo will help.

- **Have support.** Your support person may also help by giving you a gentle back and shoulder massage to help you relax. On the other hand, other mothers prefer to express in private because they feel under pressure if anyone is watching them.

A few mothers find it difficult to express, although they have a good milk supply and their babies are thriving. It is important not to judge overall milk production by the amount of milk you can express. Especially in the period just after birth, amounts expressed are sometimes thought to be a guide to actual production. This is not correct.

Expressing might not be easy when you first try it. You might feel quite discouraged if, after all your efforts, you only manage a few millilitres or even a few drops! Take heart, gradually you will become more familiar with the feel of your breasts and how to make your milk flow more easily.

Keeping things clean

When you are going to give your expressed breastmilk (EBM) to your baby, you need to be very careful that the milk stays clean and free of germs. This is even more important if the milk is for a premature or sick baby. Talk to your medical adviser or the staff caring for him about the hospital guidelines.

This is a simple guide:
- Express straight into a clean container.
- If you are going to store your breastmilk in this same container, cover it with a lid, label with the date and place in the fridge as soon as you have finished.
- Otherwise, pour the EBM into a clean container straight away, cover with a lid, label and put in the fridge. If the EBM is to be used within 6–8 hours, the room temperature is lower than 26°C and you can't use a fridge, it is safe to leave the covered container on the bench. Throw away this milk if not used within 8 hours.

How to hand express

Hand expressing is a very useful skill to learn. It is quick and you do not need any special equipment, so it can be done anywhere, anytime. While a breast pump creates suction like your baby does at the back of his mouth, when you hand express, you put pressure on the milk ducts in the breast behind the nipple to push the milk out.

You can express into any wide-mouthed container. Before you begin, wash your hands and dry them with a clean towel. Place a clean towel on your knees to catch any drips and to dry your hands if they become wet or slippery from your milk.

1. **Place your thumb and forefinger on either side of your areola,** well back from the nipple, with an imaginary line between them running through your nipple. A mirror may help if you can't see the lower part of your breast.
2. **Gently press your thumb and forefinger back into your breast tissue,** until you feel the bulk of the breast. If your breasts are full, your breast tissue might feel hard, lumpy or even a little sore. Treat your breasts gently. Expressing should not hurt. When the let-down reflex happens and the milk flows, the breast tissue softens and expressing becomes easier.
3. **Press your thumb and forefinger towards each other**, using a slight rolling action. This compresses the ducts in the breast just behind the nipple and makes the milk flow out of the nipple. Before the let-down reflex happens, the milk may only drip and you need to hold your bowl closer.

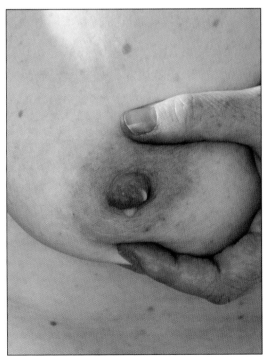 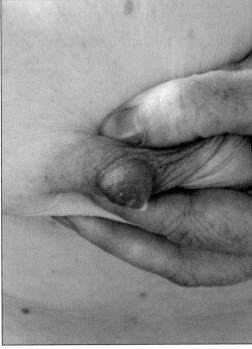

4. **Continue this compressing motion, in a rhythmical way,** until the let-down reflex happens. The milk can spray from the nipple. Several jets of milk can occur with each squeeze. The let-down reflex may take several minutes. Don't worry, the let-down is a conditioned response and will soon occur quickly each time you express.

   When you are expressing to meet all your baby's needs, you should aim to have some longer and some shorter expressing sessions. During the longer sessions you might find you will get two or more let-downs and more milk.

5. **When the flow slows, move to another section of breast,** working your way around the areola. Always place your finger and thumb on either side of the nipple. If your hand tires, you might like to use your other hand. If the flow seems to decrease, express the other breast in the same way. Change hands and breasts frequently. You will find it gets easier with practice.

   Some mothers use their right hand for their left breast and vice versa, or their left hand for the left breast and vice versa, or both hands at different times. With practice you will find what works for you. To avoid strain in your arms and shoulders, relax and change your position often.

Breast pumps

While a breast pump is not essential when breastfeeding, there may be times when it helps you to provide breastmilk for your baby. There are many different types of pumps so it is worth doing some research.

Manual breast pumps

Manual or hand pumps are popular as they are compact, not too expensive and easy to carry. They come apart for cleaning and most are fairly easy to use. You can buy hand pumps from many pharmacies and baby goods shops.

Pistons are used to create the suction. You control the amount of suction by pulling the piston. This is the safest way to produce the suction required, as it is very easy, even automatic, to release the suction if it becomes too strong. You can damage your nipple with

too much suction. There are several types of piston-style pumps. Designs that allow your whole hand to work the piston, by pulling or squeezing, rather than just a finger or thumb, tend to be more comfortable to use over a long period.

Electric pumps
Hospital-grade electric pumps can also be hired from some ABA groups, pharmacies and hospitals. When hiring a pump, you need to buy your own expressing kit that fits onto the pump. This includes the parts that come into contact with your breasts and the milk.

> **Talk to a breastfeeding counsellor before buying or hiring electric breast pumps. When hiring a pump from ABA, you will be shown how to use it and offered ongoing support from a trained breastfeeding counsellor.**

Some electric pumps have the option of single or double pumping, letting you express from one breast at a time or both together. Double pumping takes less time and some mothers feel that they get a stronger let-down, getting more milk faster. You can also express from one breast and feed your baby from the other. Your baby will trigger your let-down reflex, making it easy to express. If you are using a pump to build your milk supply from very low or nothing (relactating or inducing lactation), you are likely to need a double kit.

Even if you plan to use an electric pump, it is still worth learning about hand expressing and manual-pump expressing. Hand expressing is particularly useful to help your let-down before using the electric pump. Some mothers find they can get more out at the end of an expressing session by finishing with hand expressing.

Some electric pump kits can be used as manual pumps, at times when you are unable to use the electric pump, or after you have returned it.

How much to express

How much you express depends on your reason for expressing. If it is just to reduce engorgement when you have too much milk, you need only express enough to feel comfortable. You can hand express in a

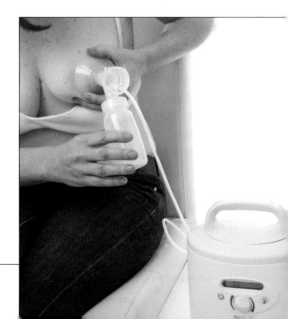

warm bath or shower, unless you want to store your milk. If you have a blocked duct or mastitis, allow baby to feed as often as possible. If your baby has not softened your breast, you can express after the feed.

How much expressed breastmilk (EBM) will be needed?

It is hard to work out the exact amount of milk needed by a baby for a feed. Babies vary widely in how much milk they normally take from the breast. If you are expressing for a baby who is premature or otherwise sick in hospital, the staff will let you know how much they want to feed him. You will be encouraged to build up your supply to what it would be if your baby was full-term.

Research has shown that the amount of milk that an exclusively-breastfed baby drinks in 24 hours doesn't really change much between 1–6 months of age. However, it varies greatly between babies, ranging from about 500 to 1000 mL (average being 750–800 mL) per 24 hours. It does not increase as the baby gets bigger. In general, the late morning and afternoon feeds may be slightly larger than other feeds. Once a baby starts eating other foods, the amount of milk he takes will gradually decrease.

To work out roughly how much milk you will need for a single feed, divide the average amount by the number of feeds your baby normally has in 24 hours. For example, using the average total intake of 800 mL, and if your baby has 10 feeds in 24 hours, then the average single feed will be 80 mL. This is a very rough guess.

> It is a good idea to express as much as you can and store it in small amounts, such as 50 mL each. Your baby can be offered a small feed and if he wants more, it is easy to take another 50 mL from storage and feed him that. This means your precious milk is not wasted.

If you regularly feed your baby with expressed breastmilk, you will get to know the amount he likes to have at a feed. This will help you to adjust the storage amounts.

If you are planning to express enough milk for just one feed to be given during your absence, you might either express a small amount (say 20–30 mL) at each feed during the day before and keep this in the fridge, or express whenever it suits you and freeze the milk. EBM should be cooled in the fridge before being added to other chilled or frozen EBM. You can express before, during, after or between feeds — whatever you and your baby find best. Some mothers express one breast at each of the first two feeds of the day and then let the baby have extra sucking time at the other breast.

When you are away from your baby at a feed time, you might need to express a full feed or just enough to keep you comfortable. Sometimes mothers are so worried about their baby's needs when planning to be away, they forget their own needs!

Wear clothing that allows you to access your breasts. Take along tissues or a small towel and perhaps extra breast pads. Breasts that become overfull can be uncomfortable and may put you at risk for blocked ducts or even mastitis. A few minutes spent expressing while away from your baby can be well worth the effort.

Containers for storing breastmilk

- **Plastic bags.** You can buy small sterile bags made for storing breastmilk from pharmacies. These are made from a special type of plastic and are thick enough to allow long-term storage in the freezer. EBM stored in these bags also thaws more quickly than when it is stored in most other containers. Other plastic bags can be used, but great care needs to be taken that they do not get punctured. Also, many are thin, so that milk cannot be stored for very long without spoiling. Chemicals may leach into the milk from some plastics.
- **Baby feeding bottles.** Glass can be cleaned easily but is more likely to break than plastic. Hard plastic can get scratched, which makes it harder to clean. Soft plastic can be punctured. When expressing for a single feed simply use what you have. Store bottles of EBM sealed with solid lids (not teats, which have holes).
- **Small glass baby food jars and other suitable containers.** It is best to use small containers, those that hold one feed or less, to avoid wastage. Avoid containers that have been used for fatty foods.
- **Special milk-storage trays.** Can be purchased or you could use clean, plastic ice-cube trays. These need to be covered and sealed well.

If you have a premature or sick baby, it is important to check with the hospital staff about containers, as they may supply them. Ask about any extra steps you should take in the handling or storing of your milk. **Breastmilk is best supplied fresh daily for a sick baby. If that is not possible, it is best used within 48 hours.**

Cleaning containers and breast pump parts

A mother's own expressing equipment does not need to be disinfected or sterilised for a healthy, term baby.

If you are expressing several times a day for a healthy baby, your expressing equipment should be rinsed well in cold water after each use to remove the milk. Store it in a clean, closed container. If you have a fridge, you may simply store the unrinsed expressing equipment in there, in a clean, closed container or plastic bag. If you cannot store your expressing equipment in the fridge between sessions, have extra parts, so you are not always rinsing and washing. This information is consistent with the NHMRC breastmilk storage guidelines as per table above. For example breastmilk may be stored for up to 6–8 hours at room temperature and up to 72 hours in the fridge.

The expressing equipment should be cleaned really well at least once every 24 hours while it is in frequent use. If the expressing equipment is only being used once a day or less, clean it after each use.

Thorough cleaning is important to make sure you have removed all milk from the breast pump parts and storage containers.

1. Wash your hands well with soap and water. Dry them on something clean — a new paper towel or a clean, unused cloth towel.
2. Take apart all containers and the breast pump so that every part can be cleaned well. Rinse in cold water to remove milk from all the parts.
3. Take care to remove all traces of grease, milk and dirt with a small amount of dishwashing liquid and hot water. Use a brush kept just for this purpose.
4. Rinse at least twice in hot water.
5. Drain bottles and containers upside-down on clean paper towel or a clean cloth towel. Cover while they air dry. Before putting away, ensure no water droplets remain in the containers or on any parts. If any water remains, dry carefully.
6. Store the dry kit in a new plastic bag, plastic wrap, more paper towel or clean, covered container until next use.

Except for the sterile expressed breastmilk bags or new plastic bags, all containers and breast pump parts used to collect or store breastmilk will need to be cleaned before use.

In areas where there are different water supplies for drinking and washing, use drinking water to wash and rinse the pump equipment.

If your baby is sick, be guided by the advice of your baby's medical team about cleaning your equipment. Also, if you and/or your baby have thrush or you have any type of infection on your nipples, you might need to disinfect your equipment after cleaning it. Talk to your medical adviser, child health nurse, lactation consultant or an Australian Breastfeeding Association counsellor for suggestions.

Handling breastmilk

Freezing breastmilk:
1. Put the lid on the container of EBM and label with the date.
2. Place the container in the coldest part of the freezer.
3. Chilled milk can be added to frozen or chilled milk as long as the container is put straight back in the freezer or fridge.

Frozen milk will expand in the container, so fill only to three quarters full, otherwise the container may burst.

Storage of breastmilk for home use

Breastmilk	Room temperature	Refrigerator	Freezer
Freshly expressed into container	6–8 hours (26°C or lower) If refrigeration is available, store milk there	No more than 72 hours Store in back, where it is coldest	2 weeks in freezer compartment inside refrigerator (-15°C) 3 months in freezer section of refrigerator with separate door (–18°C) 6–12 months in deep freeze (–20°C)
Previously frozen — thawed in refrigerator but not warmed	4 hours or less — that is, the next feeding	24 hours	Do not refreeze
Thawed outside refrigerator in warm water	For completion of feeding	4 hours or until next feeding	Do not refreeze
Infant has begun feeding	Only for completion of feeding	Discard	Discard

Reproduced with permission from National Health and Medical Research Council 2012, *Infant Feeding Guidelines*. NHMRC, Canberra p59.

Thawing and warming breastmilk

Expressed milk will separate into layers. This is normal. Just give the container a gentle shake. Strong shaking may damage the milk. Milk freezes in these neat layers, but is easily mixed once thawed.

> **Use the oldest milk first. You can thaw frozen milk in the fridge over several hours or overnight. Do not leave it to thaw at room temperature.**

Warm the container of chilled or thawed EBM in a bowl, jug or saucepan of hot water or in an electric drink heater, until milk reaches body temperature. Test the temperature by dropping a little onto your wrist. Some mothers and babies are happy to use the milk thawed but not warmed. You can also warm it quickly by moving the container about in a bowl of hot (but not boiling) water. As the water cools, add a little hot water to the bowl and keep swirling the EBM until it becomes liquid.

> **A microwave oven should not be used to thaw or heat milk, as it heats unevenly and the milk may burn a baby's mouth. It is also thought that microwaving will damage the breastmilk.**

Sometimes mothers find that their milk smells and tastes 'off' or soapy after storage in the fridge or freezer. This does not mean that the milk has 'gone bad'. It may be caused by the action of digestive enzymes that are in the breastmilk — those that break down the fats in the milk. This milk is quite safe to feed to your baby. Some babies don't like the taste. If this happens to your milk, you will have to scald your breastmilk straight after expressing to stop it happening again. This will stop the enzymes from working. To do this, heat the breastmilk to just below boiling point and then cool it quickly. One way is to place the pan in a bowl or sink of ice and water. You will only lose some of the protective properties of the milk and this is a better option than having to throw away the milk.

Transporting expressed breastmilk

Sometimes you may need to carry your EBM — between home and hospital; work and home; home and your baby's carer. This can safely be done in an insulated container (cooler bag or box) with a freezer pack or crushed ice inside. A small bottle will even fit inside a wide-mouthed vacuum flask, with ice added to keep it cool. If milk is frozen, don't allow it to defrost while being carried. If some milk does thaw, use it within 24 hours. Do not refreeze the milk.

Feeding EBM to your baby

How you feed your milk to your baby will depend on your baby's age and what he prefers. The two most common methods are a **small cup** or a **standard baby bottle**. A breastfed baby may manage a cup better than a teat and bottle if he hasn't been fed this way before. This also helps to prevent him from getting confused between the teat and your breast. Even newborns can be cup-fed.

However, a baby who has regular feeds of EBM, such as when his mother returns to the paid work force, will usually enjoy the sucking a bottle allows. If you wish to introduce a bottle and teat, don't begin until your baby has learnt to suck well at the breast and is gaining weight well.

Some older babies may only accept a bottle from a person other than their mother. However, not all babies need to have a bottle. An older baby may be happy to take the milk from his own sipper cup.

Any milk left over after the feed must be thrown away. Germs from your baby's mouth will have gone into the breastmilk. It should never be added to any other supply of stored milk.

In some special situations, a breastfeeding supplementer may be the best option. You might like to try this device if your baby is premature or ill, or if you are relactating or inducing lactation. Your baby receives milk from a special bottle, through a fine tube, as he sucks at the breast. Contact a breastfeeding counsellor for details of its use and whether it would suit you.

Pacing bottle-feeds

Breastfed babies are used to being able to control the flow of milk as they feed. They may find bottlefeeding from a fast-flowing teat quite stressful. It may look like the baby is very hungry and gulping the milk down. In fact, he might be doing all he can to swallow fast enough and not choke. One way to avoid this is to pace the feeds.

Reasons for giving babies control of the pace of feeds:

- It allows your baby to drink the amount he wants rather than the carer giving him too much.

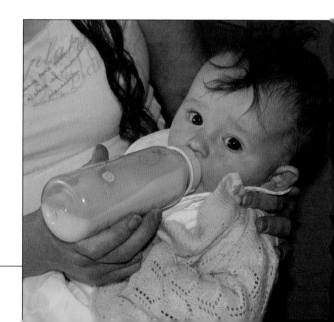

- Not giving a baby too much milk while he is away from you helps him to breastfeed better when he is with you. This will also help to keep up your milk supply.
- If you give only the amount your baby needs, you don't need to spend as long expressing to keep up with the amount of milk he is being (over)fed.

How to pace feeds — instructions for carers:
- **Do not feed the baby every time he is unhappy.** A nappy change, cuddle or more attention may be what he needs. If he is obviously hungry though, offer a feed.
- **Watch for signs that the baby is hungry** rather than feeding to a time schedule. He will get restless and may start sucking his fingers or moving his head on your chest when you pick him up. If he is past this stage, he may be crying and not stop when you comfort him.
- **Hold the baby in an upright position** when feeding him. This stops him taking too much milk at the start of the feed. Support his head and neck with your hand rather than with your arm.
- **Use a slow-flow teat.**
- **Gently brush the teat down the middle of the baby's lips,** particularly the bottom lip. This helps the baby to open his mouth wide. Let him take the whole teat into his mouth, like he would if he was breastfeeding. Do not push the teat into the baby's mouth. Let him take it himself.
- **Tip the bottom of the bottle up** just far enough for the EBM to fill the teat. As the feed goes on, you will need to let the baby gradually lean backwards more and more so that the teat stays filled with EBM. Keep his head and neck straight. At the end of the feed the bottle will be almost vertical.
- **Let the baby have rests every few minutes** to make it more like a breastfeed. This will help stop him drinking too much too fast.
- **Allow the baby to decide when to finish the feed.** He may not need to drink all the EBM in the bottle. It is better not to force him to finish it. Do not worry about wasting a small amount of EBM.

ABA's leaflet, *Caregiver's guide to the breastfed baby,* available on the website provides information to anyone caring for your baby in your absence. It contains detailed information on the thawing, warming and feeding of expressed breastmilk and the special needs of your breastfed baby.

CHAPTER 18

Working and breastfeeding

Workplace issues

Expressing milk at work

Ages and stages: the changing
needs of your baby

You can continue to breastfeed your baby when you return to paid work. Breastfeeding is not only important for her, but important for you and your employer too. Everyone wins.

- Babies who are not breastfed are more than twice as likely to be hospitalised in their first 2 years.
- Breastfeeding means fewer visits to the doctor and less time off work for you.
- It saves money.
- Breastfeeding gives a working mother a special bond with her baby that is quite different to the way her child relates to her other carers. Breastfeeding is not only very important for your baby's health, but also allows you to re-connect with your baby after time away from each other.

Workplace issues

Increasingly, employers are implementing policies that help balance family and work. These policies are not just a public relations exercise to give the company a good image. They make sound economic sense.

Whether you are fortunate enough to be employed by a family-friendly workplace or not, it is vital that you talk to your employer about your plans to combine work and breastfeeding before you go on maternity leave. This will help you both plan for the future.

Legislation

It is against the law in all Australian States and Territories to discriminate against women who breastfeed, including in the workplace. It is also against the law to discriminate on the grounds of family or carer responsibilities. Breastfeeding and family responsibilities are either protected as specific grounds in legislation or are covered by sex discrimination laws in every State and Territory.

The Australian Human Rights Commission (AHRC, formerly the Human Rights and Equal Opportunities Commission) oversees the *Sex Discrimination Act 1984 (Cth)* and is the federal body that deals with complaints relating to breastfeeding and sex discrimination. Further information can be obtained from AHRC via website: *hreoc.gov.au* or the information line 1300 656 419.

Lactation breaks

The International Labour Organization (ILO) recommends one or more daily breaks or reduced daily hours of work, counted as working time and paid at the normal rate, to allow a mother to keep breastfeeding. While many employers allow a mother to take lactation breaks, the issue of whether these breaks are paid or unpaid is generally still a matter for negotiation.

Some Australian States and Territories have passed laws to provide for paid lactation breaks for Government employees. Some individual workplaces also offer paid lactation breaks. These laws are frequently updated or changed. Check with your State or Territory Equal Opportunity Commission or the Equal Opportunity for Women in the Workplace Agency (EOWA). Also check what your workplace already offers.

Before you return to work:

- Find out your entitlements, either through the company's human resources section or through your union.
- Establish whether the company provides any other benefits, not necessarily required by law, but which may have evolved through negotiations with other employees having babies. For example, a company may not have a written policy on working from home, but may have come to some agreement with another employee whose job allows such flexibility.
- Think about how you can combine work and parenting in the best way for you, such as part-time work, or working from home for a while. While you may have more interruptions to your work day when you are breastfeeding and working at home, you will still be able to breastfeed your baby while your caregiver attends to her other needs, and you will cut travel time and expense.
- Talk to other employees with children about their experiences of returning to work and breastfeeding. Company policies may change as the needs of the workers change. A company which suddenly finds a large group of women taking maternity leave may decide to set up a special room for breastfeeding mothers to express and store their milk, if the employees point out that this will encourage mothers to return to work on schedule.

If your employer would like more information about working and breastfeeding, you could suggest ABA's Breastfeeding Friendly Workplace program.

Breastfeeding Friendly Workplaces

As there is still no national Australian breastfeeding policy for women in the paid or unpaid work force, ABA has developed the Breastfeeding Friendly Workplace (BFW) program. Consultants work with individual employers, governments and unions to tailor the accreditation to each workplace. They ensure the workplace meets the needs of breastfeeding mothers working there. The BFW program also provides other resources including interactive seminars designed to help women to plan for their return to work. Information is available on the website: *breastfeeding.asn.au/workplace.*

Expressing milk at work

Expressing and storing breastmilk are covered in Chapter 17.

If you cannot manage to feed your baby yourself during the day, you can still express your milk during your breaks and, providing that it is stored properly in thoroughly clean containers at work, you can take it home with you to store.

Workplace requirements for expressing and storing breastmilk include:

1. **Lactation breaks** — you may need time for one or more breaks.
   - Time allowed for expressing breastmilk, for lunch and other breaks — as often as baby feeds, or as many breaks as you can arrange.
   - Time to store your expressed breastmilk in a cooler bag, fridge or freezer.
   - Time to feed your baby if brought in by a carer or in on-site child care.
   - Time to take expressed breastmilk to your baby or go to feed your baby if child care is on-site or nearby.
2. **Workplace facilities** — these will make expressing and storing breastmilk safe and comfortable.
   - A clean, private, lockable room with a power outlet and comfortable chair.
   - Clean fridge/freezer or you can use a good-quality cooler bag with several frozen ice bricks.
   - Storage space for breast pump and other equipment.
   - Access to water and a sink.

3. **Flexible work options** — you may be able to arrange one or more of these to make it even easier to combine breastfeeding and work.
   - Extend your maternity leave for as long as you can.
   - Job-share or work part-time or variable work hours.
   - Work from home full-time, part-time or variable hours.
   - Work fewer hours.
4. **Support of employers and colleagues** — positive attitudes in the workplace can be very helpful.

   A positive workplace culture can make returning to work from maternity leave easier. It will be much easier if your work colleagues understand and support your efforts to continue to breastfeed rather than feeling they resent the time you spend away from your tasks.

Another word about expressing at work

Rushing out during your break to express milk for your baby while thinking about the work piling up on your desk and your boss anxious for your return, can often make it hard to trigger a let-down.

To help you relax, try a warm drink or snack, deep breathing exercises and looking at a photograph of your baby.

I expressed for several months while working as a senior lawyer in a large commercial law firm. I think I only managed to do this because I had chatted to a colleague in a similar position who had already combined work and expressing. She gave me confidence that I could do it even in our straitlaced work environment. I would block out a regular time in my diary for a meeting and disappear for the 20 minutes or so that it took — no more time than others might take to go downstairs for a coffee, chat or cigarette!

Ages and stages: the changing needs of your baby

How much you need to express and what you need to think about in making plans to return to work will depend on the age of your baby and the length of time you will be apart. Your baby will change a lot over a short space of time. Try not to worry about your 4-month-old not drinking from a bottle if you are not going back to work for another 2 or 3 months. Babies grow and learn a lot of new things very quickly.

ABA has a booklet called *Breastfeeding: women and work* and useful articles on its website. Breastfeeding counsellors are able to explore with you the many options to help you breastfeed and return to the paid workforce or study. Get a copy of ABA's leaflet, *Caregiver's guide to the breastfed baby,* to give to your child's carer. This can be downloaded from ABA's website.

Your newborn baby: birth to 6 weeks

Returning to work before your baby is 6 weeks old is not easy. Most women find they need this time to recover from the birth. New babies need feeding very often and not always at regular times. It can take 6 weeks or longer for mother and baby to get used to breastfeeding and get to know each other.

The more your baby breastfeeds, the more milk you will make, so it is important in the early days to be with your baby whenever a feed is needed. This is really only possible if you can work at home or take your baby to work with you. This helps you to be flexible about fitting work around feed times. You will find it helpful to start with a lighter workload.

Your young baby: 6 weeks to 6 months

During this period your baby will probably settle into a feeding pattern you can more easily predict. However, it is normal for babies to have some fussy periods. It is helpful to know that an exclusively breastfed baby's daily intake of breastmilk does not increase much as she grows bigger.

There are different ways to manage working and breastfeeding in this age group:

1. **Going to your baby for every feed**. You may be able to work at home, or take your baby to work. If not, you might be able to arrange for the carer to bring your baby to you at feed times. If you arrange child care close to your workplace, you could go to your baby, either on your breaks or when the carer phones you.
2. **Expressing your breastmilk** for the carer to feed to your baby while you are away. Most babies are happy to accept some feeds from the breast and others from a bottle or cup. Only introduce a bottle once breastfeeding is going well. This will help prevent nipple confusion. Once your baby is breastfeeding well and your milk supply is good, giving your baby a bottle occasionally should not affect breastfeeding.
3. **Combining breastfeeding and formula.** Your baby can be fed formula while you are away and you can breastfeed for the rest of the day, at night and on days when you are not working. Breastfeeding doesn't have to be 'all or nothing'. There are many ways you can manage.

Your growing baby: 6 months to 1 year

If being together at feed times has worked well for you, you may want to keep doing this. However, once your baby starts to have other foods and drinks, she might be happy to give up one or more daytime breastfeeds. If you are away for a short day, your baby may be happy with solid foods and drinks of water, but if you work an 8-hour day, you will need to provide expressed breastmilk or formula as well. As she begins to take solids, you may find you no longer need to express while you are at work. Expressing on weekends or at other times may provide enough of your milk to meet her needs. Let your baby breastfeed as often as she needs on your days off, before and after work and in the evenings. If you work an evening or night shift, you will want your baby to drop her night feeds, and you can boost your milk supply with extra daytime feeds.

Your older baby: 1 year plus
By this time you will probably have a routine so that your child has solids, water, expressed breastmilk or other milks while you are at work and breastfeeds when you are together. There is no need to give her formula after the age of 12 months. Most mothers find that they can continue this way without needing to express milk while they are at work. You can keep doing this for as long as it suits you both.

Choosing a caregiver
Whatever child care method you opt for, it is important to ensure that your caregiver supports your decision to give your baby breastmilk. Don't be afraid to ask any potential caregivers about their attitudes to breastfeeding, and to change caregivers if you feel you are not being supported or you are being undermined.

CHAPTER 19

Growing up

Starting solids

My baby has teeth

Weaning

These days we hear a lot about the importance of exclusive breastfeeding in the first 6 months. Breastfeeding the older child has received less attention. Many people are not aware that the World Health Organization additionally recommends continued breastfeeding, as well as other food and drinks, to at least 2 years.

Infant health authorities set no upper age limit to breastfeeding. In fact, a daily intake of just 500 mL of breastmilk can provide about one-third of the protein and energy, 45% of vitamin A and almost all of the vitamin C that a child needs in his second year of life. Until the use of infant formula became widespread, children all over the world were commonly breastfed for 2–3 years.

> Anthropologist, Katherine Dettwyler, has estimated that for humans the natural weaning age is somewhere between 2½ and 7 years.

Studies show a 'dose-response' relationship between breastfeeding and health outcomes. Breastfeeding for a short time is good; breastfeeding for a long time is better.
- The factors in breastmilk that protect the baby from disease continue to do so after the first year of life.
- Toddlers being breastfed get sick less often than toddlers who have weaned.
- IQ has been shown to be positively associated with how long a child is breastfed (even after taking other factors into account).
- Breastfeeding for 12 months or more means your child is less likely to be overweight or obese later.
- Breastfeeding for at least 12 months helps build strong bones.

Australian breastfeeding statistics show that just over one in five infants is receiving breastmilk at 12 months. However, breastfeeding into the second or third year is likely to be more widespread than this. Many mothers don't admit to feeding their older children for fear of negative comments.

Some people fear that breastfeeding an older child will make him too dependent or 'clingy'. In fact, the opposite is true. Research shows that when children form a secure attachment to their mothers through breastfeeding, they are better able to form healthy attachments to others.

Starting solids

If your baby is being breastfed according to need, your breastmilk will provide all the fluid, protein, fat, sugar, iron and other minerals and vitamins he needs for about the first 6 months of life. You don't need to begin any other food or drinks before this. In fact, if you do, your baby will take less breastmilk, your supply will decrease and you will unintentionally begin the weaning process.

Many mothers find they come under a lot of pressure from others to begin solids earlier than 6 months. But there are good reasons for waiting until your baby is 6 months old before starting him on other foods.

- Babies will not benefit from starting solids or other fluids until their bodies are ready.
- Before about 6 months, babies have a natural tongue-thrust reflex that causes the tongue to push out foreign objects. By around 6 months, they lose this reflex, making it easier for them to swallow solid food.
- A young baby is less able to cope with the foreign fats and proteins that are found in other milks, eggs, meat, vegetables and cereals. His kidneys cannot easily handle the large amount of salt found in some processed foods designed for children and adults.
- Mothers are often told to start their babies on solids so that they will sleep through the night. However, research shows that babies usually don't sleep any longer after they have started solids. Babies wake for many reasons, of which hunger may only be one.
- Exclusive breastfeeding to 6 months gives greater protection from gastro-intestinal and respiratory infections.

You should always offer a breastfeed first. Your baby will be less hungry and happier to try other foods. If he is still having lots of breastfeeds (say six or seven), try offering solid food just once a day, gradually building up to three meals. If you rush things, your milk supply will suffer. Your breastmilk is still the most vital food for him all through the first year.

A good way to begin is to have your baby sit at the meal table with other family members and allow him to play with pieces of food from your plate. He will learn about tastes and textures while learning new skills of picking up and holding food and putting it to his mouth. He will also learn that eating is a social part of family life.

It is a good idea to offer foods that contain iron, such as baby cereal or meat, as one of his first foods. Meat is particularly good as it contains zinc, which is also important. There are no rules. Different cultures have different ideas and many good foods available to them. Your own cooking is best, because it is your family diet that you want your baby to learn to enjoy. Your baby will already know many flavours from your breastmilk. Cooking his food yourself means you know exactly what he is eating.

Some babies want to be in control right from the start. If your baby is like this, you can offer finger foods until he is old enough to manage a spoon. Other babies are quite

happy to be spoon-fed, although soon they will want a spoon of their own.

Whichever way you choose, be prepared for a mess! It is easier to manage if you accept that mess is going to happen. This is all part of learning for your baby. Cover the floor under where your baby is eating with newspaper, a plastic mat or shower curtain. High chairs with trays can also catch some mess. In hot weather, dress your baby in just a nappy at meal times. It is easier to wash babies than clothes! A wrap-around waterproof bib with sleeves may also be useful. Always stay with your baby while he is eating or chewing.

My baby has teeth

While you may have read or heard that prolonged breastfeeding, especially at night, may contribute to dental caries, research shows that breastfeeding is actually protective against tooth decay. Some children may have weak tooth enamel, so special care with their teeth is required.

Some studies have shown a link between the dental status of mothers and their babies, so it is a good plan to visit your dentist to make sure your mouth is as healthy as possible. Sharing spoons or sucking on your baby's dummy to clean it can transfer decay-causing bacteria from your mouth to your baby's.

Weaning

The sucking instinct is so strong in infants that many children continue to suck dummies or thumbs well past what is normally thought of as weaning age in our society. It is common to see a child of 3 or 4 years still sucking a bottle. Is it any wonder, then, that many breastfed children enjoy the comfort, warmth and reassurance of their mother's breast for a similar length of time? The time to wean is when you and your baby want to — not when others tell you to.

It is best to follow your baby's lead. As children grow, so does their interest in the world beyond their mothers' breasts. As your baby learns about his new world, new people and new foods and tastes, he will wean naturally.

There are many advantages of breastfeeding an older baby and weaning slowly:
- Your child will be able to outgrow infancy at his own pace.
- If he is ill and refusing to eat other foods, breastmilk will provide food, protection and fluid.
- Your older child can also be weaned straight from your breast to a cup, so you won't need to bother with bottles.
- Many children who are weaned from the breast early become dependent on the bottle. They will need to be weaned from this too.

If possible, spread weaning over several weeks or months, dropping one breastfeed at a time. Weaning is a process of letting go for both you and your baby, so weaning gradually and when you are both ready is important for the physical and emotional wellbeing of both of you.

Baby-led weaning

You may be surprised to find that one day your baby makes it clear that he does not want to continue breastfeeding. He may fidget, refuse to feed or simply say that he doesn't want it. If your toddler is healthy and has shown no interest in breastfeeding for more than a few days, he is probably ready to wean. This can come as quite a shock — especially if you had planned many more months of breastfeeding. You may feel rejected and sad. You can take comfort in knowing that you have given him an excellent start to life. You may need to express over the next few days, just enough to keep your breasts comfortable. You should check for lumps that might mean blocked ducts. Your milk supply may take some time to dry up. Many women can express milk from their breasts for quite some time after their last breastfeed.

I remember feeling very sad that my son had chosen to wean. I felt great that he was ready, but I wasn't. I still get lots of lovely hugs though, where he will affectionately pat my breasts as though he's saying: 'I remember and thanks, Mum.'

Mother-led weaning

You may want or need to wean your baby before he shows that he is ready.

- You may be planning another baby.
- You may already be pregnant. Many mothers continue to feed an older child throughout their pregnancy. Some even go on to breastfeed both toddler and baby. This is quite safe. Other women prefer to wean.
- You may be returning to paid work or study and have chosen not to combine this with breastfeeding.
- You may have a medical condition for which you must take drugs that are unsafe for a breastfeeding child.
- You may be under pressure from friends or family to wean.
- You may simply have had enough.

If you are no longer enjoying breastfeeding and are feeling frustrated by your child's demands and he is healthy and happily eating other foods, this may be the time for some active discouragement. The process of weaning your baby is as personal as deciding when to wean. Much will depend on your baby's personality, his need to suck and your circumstances.

Here are some general guidelines, but overall it is best to play it by ear.

- Whether you wean your baby onto a cup or a bottle will depend on his age.
- Start by dropping the breastfeed your baby seems least interested in.
- Then, cut out one breastfeed every few days, or one each week (depending on your own comfort and your baby's response) until you are only feeding once a day.
- Be prepared to breastfeed once every second or third day for a couple of weeks to keep your breasts comfortable. If you prefer, you can hand express instead.
- Offer your baby other food and drink instead of the missed breastfeed.
- Your baby may need some extra cuddling time to help him through weaning.
- If your breasts start to feel lumpy and uncomfortable at any stage of the process, you can express a little or offer a brief breastfeed to your baby. Don't drain the breast as this will only cause more milk to be made.

If your baby is not happy about weaning, there are some things you could try:

- Offer a dummy for extra sucking.
- Give some food before a breastfeed.

- Offer only one breast at each feed and make sure he has plenty of other fluids.
- Feed to a definite routine if this is possible.
- Change daily routines to break the habit of feeding at particular times.
- Have your partner or another family member give your baby other food and drinks at his usual breastfeeding times.
- Arrange for someone else to tend to your baby at night when he wakes.

Mother-led weaning is a balance that requires you to be firm and consistent but still loving. If your child becomes ill or is distressed for any reason during the weaning process, it's best to back off for a while and start the process again later.

Weaning a toddler sometimes feels like taking two steps forward and one step back, with several false stops along the way. However, as far as we know, most children start school weaned and toilet-trained, despite their mothers' fears and frustrations.

Finding new ways to be close

Even if it was your decision to wean your baby, it can be an emotional time, especially if this is your last or only baby. While some mothers feel relieved to 'have their bodies back', others feel very sad that a special relationship has ended. Reassure yourself that you have given your baby the best and that this is the start of another exciting stage in his life and yours.

Hormones play a role in your mixed emotions at this time. After weaning, they will take a while to get back to normal. If they have not already done so, some women's periods return almost immediately, while others take a few months.

Returning to breastfeeding

Sometimes, a mother who has weaned her baby comes to regret it. She may wish to try to start breastfeeding again if:
- she or her baby may have been apart because of illness
- her baby has developed an allergy or illness after weaning
- she has adopted a baby and wants to form a special bond with him by breastfeeding. It is possible to induce lactation without having given birth.

Relactation or induced lactation requires patience, determination, time, and above all, encouragement. ABA has booklets called *Breastfeeding: and family foods; Breastfeeding: weaning* and *Breastfeeding: relactation and adoption.*

CHAPTER 20

About the Australian Breastfeeding Association (ABA)

A brief history of the Australian Breastfeeding Association (ABA)

The importance of ABA

Mothers' stories about ABA meetings

A brief history of the Australian Breastfeeding Association (ABA)

The Nursing Mothers' Association (NMA) was founded in 1964 in Melbourne by Mary Paton. When Mary's first baby was born in 1962 there was virtually no written information on breastfeeding for mothers or health professionals.

In hospital, breastfeeds were strictly timed. Babies did not room-in but were kept in the nursery and brought to the mother for feeds at set times, whether they were awake or not. Access to the breast was restricted to only a few minutes initially, slowly working up to 10 minutes each side over a number of days. Babies were routinely test-weighed after breastfeeds and regularly topped up with infant formula. After the 10 pm feed, babies were kept in the nursery and fed infant formula during the night. All of these hospital practices made it hard to establish, let alone maintain, breastfeeding.

In this climate of regimentation, conflicting and negative advice, Mary struggled to breastfeed. When, at 4½ months, she finally put her baby on formula as she had been urged, she knew that it shouldn't have to be like that. There had to be a better way.

Mary was shown a *Readers' Digest* article about a breastfeeding support group in the USA, *La Leche League*. They recommended a book called *Nursing Your Baby* by Karen Pryor. It was not available in Australia so she imported three copies. The book was a revelation to Mary and her friends. It spoke such common sense and showed successful breastfeeding as easy and natural.

A year of thinking and planning followed. Mary thought about how breastfeeding mothers could support one another and how information could be shared. On 13 February 1964, she met with five of her friends to talk and plan how to achieve her vision. Mary and these friends — Jan Barry, Glenise Francis, Pat Paterson, Pauline Pick and Susan Woods — became known as the Founding Mothers.

Deciding on a name proved to be a challenge because of the censorship restrictions at the time. *Nursing Mothers' Association* (NMA) was their final choice as it combined the ideas of breastfeeding and nurturing (the extra A for Australia was added in 1969 as the Association spread across the country).

Initially, the Association expanded by word of mouth as friends brought along their friends. Slowly the women gathered information about breastfeeding, mainly from sharing their experiences of things they had tried that had worked for them. A resource of knowledge and understanding about lactation was begun.

> **From the very beginning, the early members knew that it was important to establish their credibility with the medical profession. They enlisted the help of medical advisers who arranged NMA's first talk to the Victorian Women's Medical Society in 1964.**

Soon after, they talked to 300 Baby Health Centre Sisters in Melbourne. These medical advisers were invaluable. They arranged introductions to hospitals, medical and nursing schools, made mention of the Association in the *Medical Journal of Australia* and quietly spread the word in government circles.

In those early days there was so much to be done and no money to do it with. There was, however, tremendous drive and enthusiasm. Mothers would take bundles of newspapers, as well as their babies, to meetings as paper recycling was a key fundraiser. Dutifully washing the silver milk bottle tops and saving them for recycling was part of being a member of NMA, not to mention making cakes for the cake stalls!

Selling products was seen as being important to the financial stability and promotion of NMA. It would provide a source of income that would allow it to be independent of external funding bodies. The first NMA product to be sold was the baby sling called a Meh Tai, sewn by members. The first booklets were produced in 1969.

Starting an Association from scratch meant that much thought had to be given to its structure. Right from the outset the founding mothers knew that a code of ethics was vital. Not only would it establish the Association's credibility, but it would also keep it on track. People would not lose sight of its main aim, which was to encourage and provide support and information to mothers who wanted to breastfeed.

In May 2001, the Association voted to change its name to the **Australian Breastfeeding Association** (ABA) — a name that clearly states its purpose: to be the recognised Australian authority for breastfeeding information and support.

Mary's vision has grown from very small beginnings to the amazing organisation that ABA is today. The aims of the Association have remained the same throughout its history. That is the strength of the Association. Its other great strength is the dedication of thousands of breastfeeding counsellors and community educators, who have given countless hours of unpaid time to support other breastfeeding women and to promote widely the importance of human milk for human babies.

The importance of ABA

The work of ABA is vital as:
- a modern, dependable and accessible source of accurate breastfeeding information and support
- a lobby group, to ensure that government policies reflect the needs of families
- a support network for breastfeeding mothers and their families. ABA informs and supports them in their decision to feed their babies naturally. It gives them the knowledge and confidence to do so successfully.

At the present time (2016) there are approximately 9300 members, 1230 trained volunteers and 203 local groups throughout Australia. ABA is recognised, both in Australia and overseas, as one of the world's foremost authorities on breastfeeding.

ABA counsellors help thousands of mothers every year. They know that breastfeeding is not always easy. Their knowledge and experience can reassure mothers and help them to understand how breastfeeding works. Counsellors continually update their breastfeeding knowledge and counselling skills. However, they are not medically trained and cannot give medical advice. Their areas of expertise are breastfeeding management and mother-to-mother support. ABA has a code of ethics, which is binding upon all its breastfeeding counsellors and other members who represent ABA in any way. You can see the code on ABA's website under the tab *About>principles*.

ABA's national Breastfeeding Helpline is supported by funding from the Australian Government. It is staffed by ABA's volunteer breastfeeding counsellors who take calls on a roster system from their own homes. The system receives an average of 6500 calls a month, about 80,000 a year.

Behind the scenes, ABA counsellors and other volunteers:
- provide an email counselling service for members
- deliver nationally accredited training to ABA volunteers
- run breastfeeding education classes for parents and seminars for health professionals
- give talks about breastfeeding at hospitals and schools
- produce ABA's printed and electronic publications
- hire out electric breast pumps. This service is supported by counsellors who can help the hirer with questions about using the pump, expressing and storing breastmilk and all other aspects of breastfeeding.

- maintain ABA's website
- moderate ABA's forum
- ensure ABA is financially secure
- work with governments at all levels to advocate for breastfeeding women and their families.

These volunteer activities contribute 650,000 hours a year, worth more than $11m to the Australian economy.

Membership

Becoming a member of the Australian Breastfeeding Association (ABA) can help you gain skills, confidence and overcome challenges so you can reach your breastfeeding goals.

ABA members:

- have access to group meetings where they can receive expert assistance from trained volunteer breastfeeding counsellors and friendship and practical support from other mothers.
- have access to email counselling via our website breastfeeding.asn.au
- share in the stories of other mums and gain up-to-date information on a range of breastfeeding and early parenting topics with our member magazine Essence.
- receive our member eNewsletter. Have the latest news, information and special offers from the Australian Breastfeeding Association emailed directly to you every month.
- save hundreds of money on everyday items like food, groceries and fuel (as well as things like gifts, travel and movie tickets)with 'My Savings'.
- receive half price breast pump hire.

You don't have to do it alone! Meet new friends and have your questions answered at local get-togethers run by trained volunteer breastfeeding counsellors or educators. Whether you are fully breastfeeding, partially breastfeeding, expressing or bottle-feeding, it's great to chat to other mums and get those hints and tips that only other mums know!

As a not-for-profit organisation, the Australian Breastfeeding Association is funded primarily by membership. Your membership enables us to continue our services in supporting and educating parents, health professionals and the community about breastfeeding.

Breastfeeding Information and Research

The staff in our Breastfeeding Information and Research team provides the scientific, evidence-based information on which ABA bases its services, literature and breastfeeding policies. We provide information and resources to individuals and organisations in Australia and around the world and are regularly consulted by government and world agencies. Our services for health professionals include professional membership and *Breastfeeding Review* journal, fee for service searches and accredited continuing education in lactation management.

Mothers' stories about ABA meetings

One of the things I loved about ABA, as opposed to other mums' groups, was the like-mindedness of the other women. They made me feel welcome. There was no competition about whose baby did what first. My parenting choices were respected and appreciated. Living in a strange town where I knew no-one, I felt supported by these amazing women, who I'd never met before. The advice I got was very 'gentle' and helped me get over the problems I was having with breastfeeding my second daughter.

ABA groups are much more than other mothers' groups. You will:
- tap into the wisdom of other women
- help others, in your turn, as you gain experience
- meet people from a range of age groups and experiences — from pregnant women to mothers of five or grandmothers
- not only hear about breastfeeding but get lots of mothering/practical hints and share local knowledge
- find that meetings are moderated by someone who has been trained to do so
- make lifelong friendships.

I used to go to ABA meetings often when Sam was young. I loved going. It was so great to be surrounded by people who understood how daunting it could be in those early weeks with a new baby. What's more, they would offer to hold Sam (notorious for his reflux) while I drank a cup of coffee! I stopped going when I went back to work but I'll be back with my next one!

At ABA meetings you can see what 'normal' behaviour in a baby is and talk to other mums about how they managed. Mothers really appreciate this when they are struggling in the early weeks and later with teething babies or those who are not sleeping through the night. Contacting a local group is a great way to meet other like-minded mothers. There is often a topic that will be interesting to you. Some groups even have walking groups so you can get out and exercise safely in good company; some start play groups while others meet at shopping centres or enjoy a social night out together.

ABA groups are made up of mums who have been there and done that and know what it's like. You can see normal baby behaviour at the different ages before you go through it yourself and you can help newer mums there as well.

There are many benefits in attending an ABA meeting:
- Group meetings are fun, friendly and welcoming, especially if you are feeling a bit isolated.
- Someone will probably hold your baby while you have a cuppa while it's still hot.
- Second-time mums like coming because their toddlers can play happily with the others. No-one will judge you if your toddler 'plays up.'
- Even if the discussion topic doesn't seem relevant to you right now, most mums find they get something from the talk and you can share your knowledge with other mums (because you really are doing a great job).
- Like-mindedness — having a support network of women who agree that breastfeeding is important.

ABA groups offer two critical things: a sense of belonging and an opportunity to help others, both of which make me feel really good. I also found that the transition from being a successful liberated woman in the workforce to a grungy stay-at-home mum was a little disenchanting and soul-destroying. Then I found ABA and a new vocation. It's odd how expectant mums spend sooooo much time preparing for a birth which takes a few hours but limited time preparing for breastfeeding which lasts months, even years.

FINALLY

This book is based on the practical experiences of thousands of mothers and is firmly grounded in scientific fact. It is as simple and as complex as breastfeeding itself.

If you haven't found the answers you need, we encourage you to contact the Australian Breastfeeding Association. Its resources are far broader than it would be possible to include in one book.

This edition of *Breastfeeding ... naturally* would not be possible without the dedication and skills of many remarkable women.

- Kate Mortenson, Lactation Resource Centre Manager, who ensured our information was correct.
- Susan Greenbank, Marketing Coordinator, who worked alongside Kate and me in organising the photographic content.
- Rachel Fuller, Publications and Breastfeeding Information Portfolio Board Liaison, for her encouragement and support.
- Judy Gifford, Publications Manager, who drove the revision process and provided unwavering commitment to making this new edition a reality. Judy was assisted by members of the Proofreading and Approval Working group, in particular Joy Anderson, Dot Newbold, Elizabeth Oei, Fiona Pitt and Heather Rutherford.
- Joy Anderson for permission to use information from her articles on Diet and Weight Loss (Chapter 10) and Lactose Intolerance (Chapter 15).
- Artemiss Keyhani, Design Working Group Coordinator, who created the cover design and layout for this book, and was assisted by Debbie Court and Yvette O'Dowd in compiling the photographic content.
- The breastfeeding counsellors and other members who helped in the development of the content and in bringing it to print so beautifully.
- My three daughters, particularly Gemma, who brought the newest member of our family, Vivienne, into the world during the revision process. Having a new baby in the house has brought the needs of new parents for information and reassurance into sharp focus and has reminded me just how important breastfeeding (and this book) is to each of us.

Jill Day
Editor 2011

VISUAL CONTENT

Front cover: Amanda Radovic (main image, bottom left & bottom centre)
                and Emma Ramsay (bottom right)

Back cover: Amanda Radovic (left & centre) and Vicky Leon (right)

Thank you to the photographers and illustrators for contributing to this book.

THE PRODUCTION TEAM

Overcoming many challenges to breastfeed my daughter 4 years ago (without ABA in my life) was a herculean effort. Overcoming new problems to breastfeed my son a year ago (as a member of ABA) was a much easier task. So it was with gratitude that I worked on the design and layout of this book — often with my son at my breast.

My commitment to ABA would not be possible without the support of my loved ones. Thanks to my husband, mother and aunt who happily looked after my children. And thanks to Phoenix and Xavier, whose preciousness makes a mother want to make a difference in the world.
~ Artemiss Keyhani ~ Designer & Design Working Group Coordinator

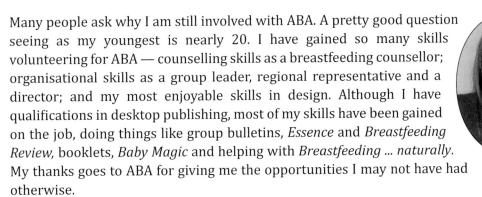

Many people ask why I am still involved with ABA. A pretty good question seeing as my youngest is nearly 20. I have gained so many skills volunteering for ABA — counselling skills as a breastfeeding counsellor; organisational skills as a group leader, regional representative and a director; and my most enjoyable skills in design. Although I have qualifications in desktop publishing, most of my skills have been gained on the job, doing things like group bulletins, *Essence* and *Breastfeeding Review*, booklets, *Baby Magic* and helping with *Breastfeeding ... naturally*. My thanks goes to ABA for giving me the opportunities I may not have had otherwise.
~ Debbie Court ~ Director and Honorary Secretary, Designer

When I joined the Nursing Mothers' Association in 1972, there was no breastfeeding book written for Australians, by an Australian. Then *Successful Breastfeeding* by Virginia Phillips was published in 1973. It was revised many times and replaced in 1996 by the first edition of *Breastfeeding ... naturally*. I have had a long involvement with ABA's publications over the years but never dreamt that I would be so heavily involved with this third edition — our first in full-colour.

It has been a wonderful experience working with everyone on this book, particularly the amazing women in my Proofreading and Approval Working Group, who have cheerfully read umpteen versions of the chapters. I also thank my long-suffering spouse who is well used to seeing me glued to the computer.
~ Judy Gifford ~ Publications Manager

Index

Index

Index

Thank you to Helen Jeffcoat for compiling this index.